BLUEBIRDS IN MY HOUSE

BONNIE AND BEN

*Bonnie and Ben—their natural beauty is rivaled
only by the beauty of their personalities.*

BLUEBIRDS IN MY HOUSE

BONNIE AND BEN

ARNETTE HEIDCAMP

with photographs
and drawings by the author

Crown Publishers, Inc.
New York

Published by Crown Publishers, Inc., 201 East 50th Street, New York, New York 10022.
Member of the Crown Publishing Group.
Random House, Inc. New York, Toronto, London, Sydney, Auckland
http://www.randomhouse.com/
CROWN is a trademark of Crown Publishers, Inc.

Printed in Hong Kong
Design by Mercedes Everett
Library of Congress Cataloging-in-Publication Data is available upon request.
ISBN 0-517-70496-X
10 9 8 7 6 5 4 3 2 1
First Edition

Acknowledgments

It is appropriate to take a small amount of space to say thank you to the people who have been helpful in one way or another during the preparation of this book.

First, a special thank-you to my husband, George, who has constructed and erected many bluebird nest boxes for me over many years, and for a million other things he has done to help me.

Next, a thank-you to both my mother and daughter for caring for or watching over the Babies each time I had to go out to buy crickets and mealworms.

Finally, to all those who have freely given leads and information, many of whom have opened up their homes and gardens to me, including Bill Curtis and Jean Krause; Eric Lawson and Karen Korff; Debbie Sheeley, Don Sweeney, and Louis DiDonna; Arlene and Frank Sheeley; Karen Jacobs; and Evelyn Rifenburg.

Also by Arnette Heidcamp

CONTENTS

BLUEBIRDS IN MY HOUSE

BONNIE AND BEN

INTRODUCTION

In February and March, winter-weary northerners anxiously await the first sign of spring, the welcomed arrival of returning Eastern bluebirds. It is said that at the turn of the century, Eastern bluebirds were as common as robins; yet today, most people under the age of forty-five or fifty have never even seen one. Some estimates have put the decline of the species' population at 90 percent. So, for many years, bluebirds have been a rare sight, indeed. Yet, in spite of their scarcity, their popularity has never diminished. There are many stunning songbirds—the oriole, the tanager, the cardinal—but none has captured the hearts of the American people as has the bluebird; and it is the most frequently mentioned of all birds in songs, on cards, and in poems as being the symbol of love, happiness, hope, and fidelity. Beauty, grace, and vulnerability combine with admirable behavior to make this mild-mannered and gentle bird one of the nation's most beloved species. In fact, four states have adopted a bluebird as the state bird, with New York having joined the ranks just within the last decades (May 18, 1970).

My own interest in bluebirds developed quite early in life when, as a child on a trip to the country, a pair was pointed out to me. I was duly impressed by the beauty of those songbirds, and the sight is surely one that I shall never forget. Later I became aware of this bird's fight for survival against all odds, and I resolved to do my share to help. For many years my husband constructed nest boxes of very exacting dimensions, and we strategically placed them in the backyard and waited in vain for that elusive bluebird that I had recalled from childhood. Fortunately, that time was not wasted—for most of those years tree swallows, beautiful birds in their own right and in the same precarious position as bluebirds, occupied the boxes to raise their young. Years later my patience and persistence would be rewarded when, finally, one day I looked up from my weeding chores and found, to my surprise and delight, a pair of Eastern bluebirds as beautiful as I had remembered, perhaps seventy-five feet away, investigating a nest box.

When Brandt Aymar, Senior Editor at Crown, asked if I'd be interested in doing something on this most revered harbinger of spring, I jumped at the chance, for not only has this gorgeous bird been a long-time personal favorite and it would give me a reason to observe them at length, but it would also give me the opportunity to spark in others the desire to join the nationwide effort to save bluebirds. While achieving such a goal is best accomplished through a knowledge of the species and its special needs, it is particularly benefited by a familiarity with specific individuals, personalities to which we can relate. The genus *Sialia* and the species *S. sialis* have been well presented in other publications. The goal here is to meet some of its members.

With that in mind, the intention was to present the birds as individuals, describing the characteristics of their personalities, and the interaction and differences between them, with emphasis on the young within each family group. To accomplish this, I would observe bluebird behavior at several locations, beginning when they usher in the spring. I expected this to yield enough information about the different families to make comparisons between juveniles within each family and the families themselves—and differences were immediately obvious, even between adults. For instance, one adult male was much shyer than the other adult males observed. What I wasn't expecting, however, was that this project would lead to foster motherhood and with it, the opportunity of a lifetime to discover the joys, firsthand and intimately, of bluebirds as individuals. Many hours were spent observing bluebirds, watching them care for their nestlings and interacting with one another. Nothing, however, could compare with helping two babies, on loan from nature, grow to become self-sufficient adults and, as a result, becoming personally acquainted with their love and devotion and the bond between them, an aspect of their personalities guaranteed to win friends and capture hearts. For to see them once surely is to not forget them, but to become familiar with them on individual bases is to love and admire them forever.

To that end, after a broad overview of the genus *Sialia* and the three species found in the United States, and a chapter on the bluebird's fight for survival, the bulk of this book is devoted to recording, in words and pictures, bluebird family life and the individuals I came to know so well.

I think there is always one special accomplishment that one aspires to achieve when he or she shares a wonderful experience with so many others. For me that goal is to present the true beauty of the bluebird, the inner beauty. I would hope to encourage others to bring bluebirds into their hearts and their lives as well by creating "bluebird-friendly" summer and winter habitats to assist them on their road to recovery. I hope, after people have become acquainted with "the Babies," there will be new converts to the bluebird recovery effort. For those new to this movement, the basics of bluebirding are covered in the Appendices, which relate to providing for bluebirds in the garden. Topics include landscaping ideas to create a summer habitat and winter refuge that will attract Eastern bluebirds to the garden; information on selecting, installing, and monitoring nest boxes, including problems and solutions; and an easy-to-prepare recipe for a peanut butter mixture (that appeals to most birds) to offer bluebirds during the harsh time of winter, when ice and snow may coat their natural food or when natural food is otherwise inaccessible.

Over the years, some of my best experiences have come through my work with birds—surely this ranks right near the top. For me, it has been a very bluebird summer, indeed.

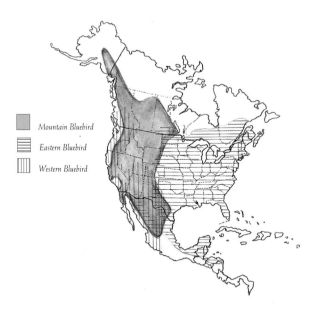

THE GENUS *SIALIA*

"Bluebird" is the common name for the three smallish songbirds constituting the genus *Sialia* of the Thrush family (*Turdidae*)—a family well noted for sweet songs. They are members of the order Passiformes, which contains several thousand highly diverse species of perching birds and the suborder Oscines, or songbirds, such as the thrushes. There are only a handful of representatives from the Thrush family in North America: the thrushes themselves, veeries, robins, and the bluebirds. Thus, the bluebird is related to the robin (*Turdus migratorius*)—probably the most well-known and abundant member of the Thrush family, a

Bluebirds appear bluest on sunniest days.

Male Eastern bluebirds are bright cobalt blue with a warm chestnut breast and white below.

relationship made obvious by the spotted breasts of both species' young. Early settlers to the colonies referred to bluebirds as "blue robins" because the birds reminded them of the beloved robins of their homeland. Britain's robin is a rather small, tame, and familiar bird of parks and gardens. It sports a red breast similar to the bluebird's, which it uses as a badge in its territorial defense, and resembles the bluebird more than our robin.

Bluebirds may be found throughout the United States and much of Canada and Mexico. In fact, one bluebird species or another is found in every state of the United States except Hawaii. The Eastern bluebird (*Sialia sialis*) nests throughout eastern North America from southern

Canada, as far west as Saskatchewan and the Great Plains states, south to eastern New Mexico. They winter in the southern part of their breeding range and south as far as Mexico and Nicaragua.

The Western bluebird (*Sialia mexicana*) is the western counterpart of the Eastern bluebird and, in fact, their ranges overlap in the Southwest. They nest in western North America from southern British Columbia, east to the Rockies and south to southern California and western Texas to south-central Mexico. Except during breeding season, the Western bluebird travels in flocks and is the least migratorial of the three species. Its movements tend to be more by altitude than by latitude, with wintering at lower elevations, where it is common in desert-area mesquite groves.

The most migratorial of the three species and the largest, the mountain bluebird (*Sialia currucoides*), nests at elevations up to 12,000 feet in the foothills and mountains of western North America from east-central Alaska, east to southwestern Manitoba and the Dakotas, south to southern California, northern Arizona, and southern New Mexico. While some may winter as far south as Mexico or as far north as British Columbia, the primary wintering grounds are the plains and agricultural areas at lower elevations throughout the middle and southern portions of the breeding range in the Southwest.

Bluebirds have a very distinctive appearance, being one of only a few North American birds that are primarily blue. The blue coloring of their feathers is structural and a bird's brightness directly relates to the amount of available light. Thus, the birds appear bluest on the sunniest days. But birds and animals tend to see the short wavelengths of light constituting sunlight—the blues—rather poorly. So what stands out to us and looks spectacular may very well be a benefit to the bluebird, an adaptation making them less visible to mammalian and avian predators on their open and exposed habitats. Albinism, a genetic defect that stops or inhibits the enzyme (hyrosinase) responsible for pigment (melanin) production, although rare, has been reported among all three species of bluebird. It is least common, however, in the mountain bluebird.

Each of the three species of *Sialia* is a different shade of blue. The male Eastern bluebird has bright cobalt upper body plumage, including the wings and tail; warm chestnut-colored throat, breast, and flanks; and a soft white belly and undertail coverts. Except that the female has a conspicuous white eye-ring and her wings and tail are bright blue, her overall color is similar to that of the male but more drab, grayer above and pale rust to whitish below. A nonmigratory subspecies residing in the mountains of southeastern Arizona is paler overall.

The male Western bluebird is somewhat darker than the Eastern male, sporting deep purplish-blue upper body plumage, including wings and tail, with a chestnut-colored patch of variable width across its back. Unlike the Eastern bluebird, the throat is blue, never chestnut or rust. The belly is a grayish blue. The female is duller overall than the male, with a grayish throat, brownish on the back, and very pale rust on the breast and flanks. Her tail and wings show some blue.

The male mountain bluebird is entirely sky-blue with the color deepest and brightest on the upperparts, wings, and tail. The female has bright blue wings, tail, and rump, but otherwise is grayish brown. Her belly and undertail coverts are white and she has a conspicuous white eye-ring.

Juveniles of all three species are gray-brown on the back and head; the breast is gray-spotted white, and color appears on the wings and tails. The three species of bluebird are similar in song, as well—a rich warble for both the Eastern and Western, and an infrequently heard, short warble for the mountain bluebird.

Bluebirds are creatures of open habitats, preferring orchards, fields, farmlands, and forest and woodland edges. With less stringent nesting requirements than the other species, the mountain bluebird also prefers such open habitats as rangelands, sagebrush plains, mountain

The female is similar to the male but more drab.

Juveniles are gray-brown and spotted but show some color on the wings and tail.

meadows and pastures up to the timberline, aspen and cottonwood groves, and riparian valleys. These areas of widely scattered trees and shrubs among grasses and forbs harbor the caterpillars, beetles, grasshoppers, crickets, and spiders that form the bulk of the bluebird's diet during nesting season. The winter diet contains more berries. Insects and spiders are taken if and when available, but when it becomes so cold that there are none, they may live entirely on a wide variety of berries, such as sumac, possum-haw (but only after several freeze-thaw cycles), dogwood, or honeysuckle. (See Appendix I for a detailed list of berry-producing trees, shrubs, and vines attractive to bluebirds.)

Foraging behavior for the Eastern and Western bluebirds is quite similar. They perch on a fence, in a shrub, or on some other such vantage point above the ground in a hunched position, waiting to catch sight of a potential meal—which they are able to spot at distances up to seventy-five feet—before making short forays to the ground to capture it. The mountain bluebird perches in more of a horizontal position than the other two species, and it tends to hover above its prey before dropping down to the ground to grab it—a likely adaptation to the lesser number of available perching sites over their favored habitats. Although the others can and will, the mountain bluebird is more inclined to capture insects in flight.

THE FIGHT FOR SURVIVAL
AND HUMAN INTERVENTION

*Nothing is more common in Pennsylvania than to see large flocks of these birds
in spring and fall, passing, at considerable heights in the air, from the south in
the former, and from the north in the latter season.*[1]

When I moved to upstate New York, I began inquir-
ing about where the bluebirds were, only to find that
the only blue bird that most people had ever seen was

---

1. Alexander Wilson and Charles Lucian Bonaparte, *American Ornithology: or the
Natural History of the Birds of the United States* (Philadelphia: Porter and Coates). This trea-
sure, located by a friend, was published after Wilson's death in the 1800s, not earlier
than 1825, the latest date mentioned in the book. It is difficult to determine when it
was written specifically but it undoubtedly spanned a period of time during the early
1800s. The book is prefixed with the *Life of Wilson*, who died in 1813 of dysentery.

the bluejay. "They just disappeared," I was told, but the "old timers" remembered them. The property next door to me had once been known as Bluebird Farm because so many bluebirds had nested in fence-post cavities among

Ideal bluebird habitat is open land with scattered trees.

the grapevines there. I wanted to know what the factors were that contributed to such a sharp decline over so short a period. While some reasons were natural, of course, most, unfortunately, were human-inspired.

The primary contributing factors—loss or destruction of habitat and the inability to find suitable nesting sites—directly or indirectly relate to human activity. The bluebird is a cavity nester—that is, it builds its nest, lays its eggs, and raises its young in natural tree and other cavities such as tree snags and rotted-out tree limbs and fence posts. However, the bluebird does not excavate the cavities itself. Instead it is a secondary user, utilizing abandoned or surplus cavities already created. North American woodpeckers are primary cavity nesters, excavating mostly in snags that may ultimately become home to a bluebird family. Although these woodpecker-hollowed cavities are relatively safe from predators and afford good protection against the elements, they are in short supply and the competition for them is fierce. Suitable housing might be more available in undisturbed forest, but forest does not provide an appropriate habitat for the bluebird. Ideal bluebird habitat is open land with scattered trees, such as an orchard, field, or farmland.

It might well be argued that, in general, the bluebird population is cyclical, crashing periodically as a result of harsh winters, followed by a rebuilding of the numbers during subsequent milder ones. And a case may very well be made that the Eastern bluebird population had fluctuated for years as a direct result of human activity with no long-term ill effects. At first, when settlers cleared vast numbers of oak and chestnut trees for farming, the bluebird population probably increased. But after the Civil

War, there was a change in agricultural practices, with settlers moving westward to the prairie. Eastern farmland
reverted back to forest, and bluebird numbers may have
declined to the pre-settler level along the eastern portion
of the country. Later, around the turn of the century, when
mature trees were being cut to supply firewood and building material to major Eastern cities, conditions once again
existed that favored a bluebird population increase in rural
areas. It is noted that, around that time, bluebirds were a
very common songbird. Afterward, however, that situation
quickly turned around—there was no more rebounding;
the numbers spiraled downward. What happened?

THE TRAGIC DECLINE

Social and economic changes in our country were rapidly
coming to a boil by the time of World War II. Coincident
to those changes, a tragic decline that had already begun
to occur among bluebirds was nearing a crescendo.
There was a human population explosion after the war,
with the tendency for people to move en masse from
cities to rural areas and then set about to "improve" their
new homes. Rural orchards, farmlands, and pastures—
prime bluebird habitat—became subdivisions, shopping
malls, parking lots, and highways to reach them.
Wooden fences with hollowed-out posts and their accompanying blackberries and pokeweed were replaced with

maintenance-free metal and chain-link, and old, rotted trees with natural nesting cavities were cut down for aesthetic or economic reasons or at least low-hanging, hollowed-out limbs were removed in an attempt to keep everything neat, clean, and meticulous.

In addition to people's usurping prime bluebird habitat, an invasion of another kind had taken place. Starlings and house sparrows—two aggressive cavity nesters imported from England in the latter part of the last century and now widespread—were competing with the bluebird for its nesting sites—and winning. Eggs were pierced, nestlings were killed, and the mild-mannered nesting bluebirds themselves were evicted by the pushy immigrants. With all the interloper activity, both human and avian, bluebirds were experiencing a nesting-site catastrophe. It had been going on for years, but now, with the concurrent shortage of suitable habitats, they became unable to recover. With nowhere for the birds to go, bluebird numbers declined critically.

Another factor with damaging effects on bluebird population—of which, I admit, I have seen little written—is the use of pesticides. Bluebirds, as well as other birds, are subject to the effects of chemical poisoning, either by direct contact with the agent—as, perhaps, when used on lawns—or by ingestion of pesticide-coated insects. In the 1950s, insecticides probably reached their pinnacle of popularity. With farmers' use of pesticides to kill such crop-damaging enemies as cutworms, they inadvertently affected a major cutworm predator in the bluebird, for it is now known that certain pesticides, such as DDT, cause thin, weak eggshells that are frequently crushed during incubation. So by the 1950s, bluebirds were being bombarded with deadly chemicals.

To add insult to injury, several harsh winters dealt a devastating blow. The winter of 1957–58 was unusually cold in the South, and thousands of songbirds that winter there starved or were frozen to death. Hardest hit by the catastrophic weather were the bluebirds. Trees and shrubs were covered with ice, freezing rain, or snow much of the winter. With ice and freezing rain coating the berries, natural food became unavailable and the bluebird population was drastically reduced even further. Frozen bodies were found throughout the bluebird's main wintering range, with estimates that up to 50 percent of the population had perished. Six more harsh winters followed that disastrous one, with unusual cold killing more bluebirds each year until, by 1963, the population reached its lowest point ever. Bluebirds were in danger of extinction.

HUMAN INTERVENTION
Horrified by the plunge in the bluebird population, people began to take action to help the bird restore its

numbers. The most beneficial help offered by humans was the "bluebird trail," which, quite simply, is a series of nest boxes placed at suitable intervals in areas inhabited by bluebirds. To that end, publicity was a great impetus. An article in *National Geographic*[2] alerting readers to the bluebird's plight and a possible solution created an outpouring of emotion across the nation. Many sympathetic bird lovers pledged their help.

The use of nest boxes to bring bluebirds close is not a new concept and is reflected in the following quotes on the Eastern bluebird (grouped with the warblers and referred to as "blue-bird (*Sylvia sialis*)") from Alexander Wilson's *American Ornithology*:

> . . . visiting the box in the garden, or the hole in the old apple-tree . . .
>
> . . . few farmers neglect to provide for him, in some suitable place, a snug little summer house, ready fitted and rent-free.[3]
>
> And all that he asks is, in summer a shelter.[4]

Wilson's work, written nearly two hundred years ago, makes it obvious that our love affair with the bluebird, even to the extent that nest boxes were provided, is not

2. Lawrence Zeleny, "Song of Hope for the Bluebird," *National Geographic* 151, no. 6 (June 1977): pp. 854–65.

3. Wilson, *American Ornithology*, pp. 159–160.

4. Ibid., p. 161.

a new phenomenon. People had been setting up bluebird nest boxes specifically to counteract the nesting-
site shortage caused by sparrows and starlings at least
since the 1930s. A pioneer in this concept was Thomas E.
Musselman of Quincey, Illinois, who coined the term
"bluebird trail" for the twenty-five boxes he placed along
country fence posts in Adams County. Dr. Musselman
made note of severe spring weather that had killed thousands of bluebirds near the turn of the century, and
noticed that there were fewer natural nesting sites available, with a corresponding increase in the number of starlings and sparrows. And armed with the knowledge of
how well house wrens (*Troglodytes aedon*) had proliferated
with the construction of birdhouses, Musselman envi-
sioned a similar benefit to bluebirds. He experimented
with several types and concluded that plain boxes with
one entrance hole were preferred. Musselman encouraged
the erection of boxes throughout the countryside. This
later became known as a bluebird trail, and his idea
formed the basis for all future plans to save the bluebird.

Possibly standing out above all others recently
is Lawrence Zeleny, a retired agricultural biochemist
from Maryland, who saw triumph in adversity and
launched a crusade to save this beautiful and imperiled
songbird from extinction. Founder of the North
American Bluebird Society, Lawrence Zeleny was *the*

champion for bluebird conservation following his retire-
ment from the Beltsville Agricultural Research Center in
1966. When Zeleny saw a pair of bluebirds at the center,
he recalled how until 1950, when the starlings invaded,
there had been many bluebirds there, and he placed one
box outside his office window and monitored its
progress. Later, when he retired from Beltsville, Zeleny
erected more boxes at the center and fledged twenty
bluebirds the first year and eighty the second. He
encouraged others to do likewise, and that encouragement is at the root of most bluebird trails today. Soon he
had a following of bluebird enthusiasts to join his efforts,
and trails sprang up across not only the breeding range of
the Eastern bluebird but the Western and mountain
species as well. Zeleny, who was born in Minnesota in
1904 and died of a heart attack in May 1995, will always
be remembered as the preeminent bluebird conservation-
ist of our time.[5]

OTHER WAYS TO HELP

People may have inadvertently given a helping hand
to the bluebird in more ways than one. Nest boxes have
helped tremendously to counteract the shortage of natural nesting sites. But an added benefit of providing

5. John Boon, "Dr. Lawrence Zeleny—An Odyssey of Love," *Sialia* 17,
no. 3: p. 85.

artificial nesting sites is that bluebirds will roost in the
boxes for protection from bad weather. Individual birds
numbering a dozen or more have been found huddled
together in a nest box, keeping one another warm
during severe winter weather. Roosting boxes are very
similar to nesting boxes, except that the entry is near the
floor of the box rather than near the top and there are
staggered perches on which to roost. The difference in
design is based on the principle that warm air created by
the bird's body heat is lighter than cold air and will rise
to the top of the box and become trapped, thus providing a warmer microclimate. Of course, there are no ventilation holes at the top of the roosting box and some
folks even have built thicker walls, sandwiching a layer of
styrofoam between the outer wall and an inner wall of
thin wood, such as luan, to provide additional warmth.
However, when considering roosting boxes versus nest
boxes, remember that a nest box allows the bluebirds to
huddle together for communal warmth at the bottom of
the box, with the entry hole away from them. The ventilation holes at the top of the nest box should be plugged
up for the winter and removed for the spring nesting season if the box will be used for roosting.

When natural food is inaccessible, or even as standard
winter fare, mixes containing fats and protein may be
offered to the bluebird (as well as most other birds) to

help soften the harshness of the season. My favorite recipe consists of peanut butter, flour, and cornmeal added to melted vegetable shortening such as Crisco, and then enriched with chopped nuts and raisins, currants, or berries. The mixture can be packed into suet holders or crumbled and left on a picnic table or some such place where it is conveniently available to the birds.

The mixture, which appeals to most birds, can be used year-round without concern of spoilage. When it is offered in the spring and summer, woodpeckers, cardinals, mockingbirds, and robins feed it to their young, and orioles absolutely adore it. The recipe can be found at the back of this book (see Appendix III).

ON THE ROAD TO RECOVERY

Bluebirds are making a comeback. According to a recent U.S. Fish and Wildlife Service report,[6] people who feed and house birds play a vital role in the recovery of bluebirds and other songbirds and, as a result of human intervention, Eastern bluebird populations have increased more than 2 percent per year since 1966.

The increase in the bluebird population is a remarkable success story. It is the direct result of widespread action by sympathetic bird lovers who pledged their help

6. "Backyard Birds Get Boost (Birding Briefs)," *Birder's World* 9, no. 4 (August 1995): p. 12.

and followed through. Caring, dedicated, and sympathetic people joined together in an unprecedented recovery effort. Single nest boxes and organized trails
sprang up across the United States and Canada, with one
in excess of 2,000 miles long. Bluebirds by the thousands
are fledging annually from these boxes, and more boxes
will need to be added to the trails to accommodate the
burgeoning population. It doesn't matter whether the
individual's role has been major or minor; together, people have been effective.

The bluebirds are making a comeback, but the causes
of their decline haven't changed much. Natural nesting
sites on suitable habitats are still in short supply, and
competition for them will remain keen. Bluebirds have
become dependent upon us, and we must never forget
our commitment to them. It is simple. We must create a
summer habitat conducive to nesting success, complete
with pesticide-free open areas for hunting and cavities
for raising young. And we must offer a winter refuge by
landscaping to provide food, water, and shelter during
the extreme weather of winter (see the Appendices for
suggestions). If we continue to provide for the bluebirds,
we will have them forever.

LIFE OF THE BLUEBIRD

As summer comes to a close we notice many changes around us, but even before the autumnal equinox arrives, invisible changes are under way in the marvelous annual cycle of nature. The trees' leaves have become dull—no longer vibrant, they look old and worn. Drought, high daytime temperatures, cooler evenings, and decreasing day length are not conducive to the production of new growth. While it will be some time before all visible life is drained from them, many trees and shrubs begin to harden off in preparation for the winter ahead. With nesting chores for the year finished, bird song no longer fills the air. This is not an abrupt change, for the birds had been stealing away one by one since spring; it's just that one day we realize they are gone.

For the bluebirds, changes are also under way. Decreasing day length initiates certain glandular activity. Hormonal changes cause the gonads to shrink to pre-breeding size and the birds become less territorial, wandering freely. Bluebirds maintain very strong family ties throughout summer and fall, and their numbers are at the highest level at that time of the year. But as colder weather approaches, bluebird families join together and form loose flocks. These flocks may join other flocks. Some of them will migrate, pushing just far enough south to escape the harshest weather of winter. At a time when insects are less abundant and berries are most plentiful, bluebirds add more energy-producing carbohydrates to their diet. The sugars in those berries will be converted to the heat energy they will need for warmth.

Bluebirds molt in late summer, while protein-rich insects are still plentiful and energy-giving fruits are available in abundance to meet the demands of the molting process. At this time each year, adult birds undergo a gradual replacement of all their feathers. For their first molt to adult plumage (which may start as early as July to be completed by fall), juvenile bluebirds replace only contour feathers; the feathers of the wings and tail, which grew in while the birds were nestlings, are kept until the following year.

ON THE EDGE OF WINTER—IN SEARCH OF FOOD

During the nonbreeding season, bluebirds wander freely in search of food and are seen in places they wouldn't be found during nesting season. Their intense, rich blue coloring stands out against the tawny yellows and soft golds of the dried-up grasses and forbs, the brown of leafless trees and shrubs, or the white of snow. Excitement wells up; people call the local radio station to make the announcement, they feel so personally privileged and proud to have seen the elusive bluebird.

The bluebird wintering range is roughly the southern two-thirds of their breeding range, but moving south for the winter is not a hard fact of bluebird life, for even those who do move southward don't truly migrate. There are no set routes, patterns, or departure dates, and it is likely that there are no set wintering sites, either. As insects become scarce, bluebirds rely heavily on fruits and berries. Unfortunately, flocks of greedy starlings frequently strip the trees and shrubs bare, leaving the bluebirds no choice but to move on. The flocks just drift from one area to the next, always on the edge of winter in search of food, whether it is grasshoppers, crickets, and spiders—their fare of choice—or wild grapes, rose hips, and dogwood berries. It may even be human offerings in the form of suet or mixtures containing suet, peanut butter, berries, raisins, or currants. Banded bluebirds from New York and Pennsylvania have turned up in Florida, while birds banded in New Hampshire and Massachusetts have appeared in Georgia and the Carolinas.

Staying just ahead of winter has its benefits: the high energy requirements and risk of mortality associated with a long migration are eliminated and the birds return sooner to their breeding ground, ahead of competitors. But there is also a price to be paid for living so precariously. The uncertainties of winter can wreak havoc on bluebird numbers, and the species experiences periodic population crashes during harsh winters. Happily, with a couple of good winters—providing weather is the only factor—the numbers rebound.

In sharp contrast to the preceding year, the 1994–95 winter was mild in the Northeast—a far cry from the forty-two major storms that had been predicted in the *Farmers' Almanac*. In such mild winters, there are bluebirds around for the entire season. Migration is weather related, and in some years the birds may be absent only from mid-December to mid-February. They travel only as far south as is required to find food. In early January 1995, I made a trip to Five Rivers Environmental Education Center at Delmar, New York, just west of Albany, to see a wintering flock of bluebirds; similar flocks were seen in this area later in January and in February, as well. A ridge in the jet stream kept the Northeast mild through the end of January, but ironically, winter kicked in with a vengeance a mere two days after Puxatawny Phil predicted that spring "is just around the corner." Even so, the ice and snowstorms never materialized, and some bluebirds were seen in northern areas for the entire season.

HARBINGERS OF SPRING

On their wintering grounds, whether or not they migrate, bluebirds lead a somewhat nomadic existence, traveling in flocks or family groups to sun-drenched areas where there may still be some insects or to stands of fruit trees and shrubs where there are berries. But late winter's lengthening days and warmer sun seem to stir thoughts of nesting. Before spring arrives, the flocks have broken up and bluebirds in the South have started nest-building while individuals farther north have arrived on their territories. Some first-time breeders, however, may not return until much later. As is the case with so many migrating birds, males tend to return to their breeding grounds first in order to select suitable nesting sites to offer the females. But the returning bluebirds may also arrive in pairs or groups. When a male and female arrive together, they are a pair from the previous season. Successful pairs may even stay together until one of them dies. Previously paired birds still go through the courtship ritual, although they do it a little more quickly. When several birds return together, they may or may not have migrated. In any event, the flock will soon split into pairs.

As I sat in my backyard, a beautiful, sparkling blue male flew in from the wooded area in the rear to the new nest box in the middle of the lawn, as though he had already known of its location. From my position it was difficult to tell if a female had accompanied him—perhaps he was merely claiming the box. He sat on the top of the box, fluttered and waved his wings in display, and sang. If he had been advertising for a female, his song would have been more robust and it would have been delivered from an exposed branch near the top of one of the trees. After a few moments, the male flew to one of the shrubs to the south of the box, sang some more, and then returned again to the box. He repeated this behavior from different small trees and shrubs along the perimeter of the lawn containing the box. "He's mapping out his territory," I thought. Then he flew to the apricot tree and, in addition to giving his song, he flew down to the ground, picked up something to eat or a token piece of nesting material, and brought it to the box. Perhaps the female *had* accompanied him and he was trying to convince her to accept him, his offerings, and the house he had chosen.

Bluebird courtship is a very gentle affair in comparison to the displays of many other songbirds, with the northern, more migratorial individuals far more demonstrative than their southern relatives. Courtship is centered on and directly involved with the selection and approval of the nest site. When the male locates a potentially suitable cavity, he sings a gentle warble to the female while going in and out of the home he hopes to sell her, stopping only to bring her gifts—some tasty morsels or bits of nesting material—in an attempt to entice her to accept him and his selection. She sits passively by, taking it all in, and may even resist his overtures for as long as several days before finally giving in and inspecting the site offered. When and if she relents, the male becomes ecstatic and his song erupts into a new richness as he flutters around and around his mate, showing off in absolute excitement. If his offering is rejected, he must continue the search until he locates a home that she finds acceptable. I watched one amorous male cling to the front of the nest box and poke his head in and out of the hole. He appeared to be acting out the feeding of babies in order to pique the female's interest.

THE HABITATS

I visited several sites containing nesting pairs of bluebirds. Interestingly, the habitats ranged from small, not-too-open sites with some mowed lawn that were adjacent to wooded areas, to open fields with no small trees or shrubs from which to hunt. All sites had some

Bluebirds at the Road Site built in a nonstandard nest box.

open areas and all but one had some small trees. All the sites I observed contained a mixture of the large deciduous trees common to Eastern forests—maples, oaks, and so on, as well as some evergreens. Most of the sites had more than one nest box, the majority of which were occupied by a friendly competitor, the tree swallow (*Tachycineta bicolor*). In a recent study,[1] the researchers' findings did not support their prediction that the onset of nesting activities is earlier on sites with multiple nest

1. Jonathan H. Plissner and Patricia Adair Gowaty, "Eastern Bluebirds Are Attracted to Two-Box Sites," *Wilson Bulletin* 107, no. 2 (June 1995): pp. 289–95.

The resident tree swallows would sit on the bluebird nest box at the Garden Site.

boxes. However, my experience was breeding, and nesting behavior occurred earliest at the site where tree swallow nesting activity was in progress early in the season—at least two weeks earlier than sites where tree swallows were absent or claimed boxes later.

THE ROAD SITE — One area I visited had many fruit tree saplings and some medium-size deciduous trees and was surrounded by woods. Grape vines bordered the rural road and the property had a small to moderate amount of traffic passing by. There was more human activity at this site than at the others, particularly right across the road from the nest box, as well as a large dog who barked every time I was there.

As they had in many prior years, the bluebirds at this site built in a "nonstandard" bluebird nest box mounted eight to ten feet high, directly adjacent to the road. Here, the parents did much hunting on the road's shoulder as well as along the roadway itself, and more from telephone wires than from any other vantage point. Insofar as bluebirds may stake out and claim large, open areas from which to hunt, and the competition at this site from many other pairs of nesting birds was strong, the Road Site was a bit of an enigma, yet bluebirds have successfully fledged broods from this site for many years. The resident tree swallows began nesting earlier here than the bluebirds, and they were vigorous about defending the space around their nest box. If one of the bluebirds landed within eight feet of a tree swallow box, it was chased immediately. While the female bluebird took the hint, the male would go back over and over again, almost deliberately to annoy the tree swallow. The male at this site exhibited much abrasion of the tail feathers and was generally less attractive—if that is possible—than males observed at other sites.

THE GARDEN SITE — At the opposite end of the spectrum, the Garden Site was very, very open and quiet. Here, the area consisted primarily of overgrown field and a large mowed area. A few newly planted ornamentals were a good distance from the nest box, while large deciduous trees were a considerable distance away and did not figure in bluebird activity while nesting. But there was also a large vegetable garden. Hunting emanated primarily from the nest box or from the wooden fence surrounding the garden on which the nest box was mounted, but occasional forays were made to the mowed area. The garden, frequently watered, seemed to yield the most—to other birds as well. Although I did not observe it personally, I understand that there were times, even during the nesting season, when five or six hunting bluebirds might be counted there. One of the resident tree swallows would sit on top of the bluebirds' nest box from time to time, but neither the male nor the female ever made any attempt to drive it away. The birds at this Garden Site were very attractive, but they tended to be shier than birds at the other sites.

THE POND SITE — My favorite site contained two good-size ponds, a variety of tall trees that cast high shade, some shrubs, and several young understory and ornamental trees from which the birds might perch and hunt. It was an oasis in the middle of a sprawling industrial and shopping mall setting, not far from an urban area. The birds at the Pond Site were observed to cling to the trunks of trees more often than birds at the other

The birds at the Pond Site cling to the shagbark hickory trees.

sites, and their favorite trees for that purpose were the shagbark hickories (*Carya ovata*).

Tree swallows repeatedly skimmed the pond for insects at this site. One pair had taken up residence in a box at the pond's edge, but it was not uncommon to see six or eight hunting there. The bluebirds basically ignored the swallows, and occasionally the male would sit on top of the tree swallows' nest box, but there were never any altercations. Both parents were attractive. The female was totally oblivious to any human activity around her, while the male was only slightly bothered.

Accompanying the female during nest building is more than just a loving ritual.

COURTSHIP AND NESTING

By late March, bluebirds began making appearances at the various nesting sites in our area and by early April, site selection was well under way. The male examines many potential sites, investigating all possibilities, natural and man-made. Natural secondary cavities are in short supply these days, especially in bluebird habitat, so the possibility exists that many bluebirds will never see anything but man-made nest boxes. That situation may have already, or soon will, result in bluebirds' losing inherited information about natural sites—

that's evolution at work. The upside to this development is that nest boxes are safer from predators and are more amenable to insect control. They are usually better insulated from heat, cold, or rain and are better ventilated, cleaner, more ideally situated, and exclude the entry of starlings. Fledging success, therefore, is predictably greater in man-made nest boxes than in natural cavities.

Bluebirds may make many false starts, however. When attention to a particular box makes you think that the box had been chosen, the birds may surprise you. At the Road Site, which was also the earliest site to see bluebird activity, attention had been given to three different boxes but primarily to the one at the end of the row. When it appeared that the birds had, in fact, chosen that box, they made an abrupt switch to the one in the middle. Such behavior—effectively claiming all the boxes in his territory—may be the male's way of discouraging other nesting birds.

In upstate New York, we are not blessed with the long, leisurely spring of the South. The brief Northeastern season begins later and is increasingly compressed the farther northward one travels. While we may look for bluebirds early, nesting cannot truly begin until suitable nesting material and food are available—and that means not until the snow has melted. Even though boxes had been chosen, it would not be until late April that most nest building would commence and not until early May before any egg laying started.

THE HONEYMOON — Once they agree on the new home, the bluebird pair remain in the vicinity, defending their selection, until the female begins nest building. Usually an intruder can be chased from a claimed territory, but occasionally bluebirds fight with other bluebirds over nesting sites. When that happens, the battles can be vicious. It is always males defending against other males, while females fight with other females. This period of time is commonly called "the honeymoon," and may last several weeks.

During the honeymoon, the bluebird pair form a strong bond that will prepare them for their impending parental duties and will endure for the entire nesting cycle. There is frequent activity at the nest, particularly in the morning, with much time spent going in and out, just checking things. The birds perch near or directly next to one another and vocalize. He brings her food. If they are hunting or otherwise become separated, they call back and forth to one another, staying in constant contact by sight or sound. But there may be an ulterior motive here, for out of sight is out of mind, and when out of contact, one or the other might mate with another bird. DNA analysis has shown that some eggs in a clutch may be from a different father or mother from that of the bond pair! When an egg has a different mother, it is because another female—probably a "floater" with no nest or mate of her own, whether she mated with the resident male or a floater male—has left an egg in the box of the resident pair. This "egg dumping" may account for the occasional sixth egg in a clutch, a white egg in a clutch of normally blue eggs, or an infertile egg in an otherwise fertile clutch. There are genetic benefits to this infidelity, including, I'm sure, the constant introduction of fresh genetic material.

Once the pair have formed and cemented their bond, nest building will begin. The task is almost exclusively undertaken by the female. While the male may bring token bits of material, a piece of grass, or a pine needle, his primary contribution is a soft song of encouragement while she gathers materials. Accompanying the female is more than just a loving ritual, however; it serves the dual purpose of protecting her from predators and preventing rival suitors from mating with her.

The main ingredient in nest construction depends upon what materials are most common in the vicinity and available closest to the site. Whatever material is used —grasses, pine needles—the nest is neatly constructed, generally three to four inches deep with the cup portion just under two and one-half inches in diameter and about two and one-quarter inches deep. (The nest at the Pond Site was only about two and one-half inches high.) Slow and meticulous, the female starts by poking longer, coarser pieces of her chosen material into the cavity. She molds a cup with her breast and then lines the cup with finer grasses. Typically, the nest will be completed in five or six days, although it may take twice that long. On the other hand, birds in a hurry have built nests in much less time— even as little as one day. Copulation generally begins concurrently with nest building and ceases when incubation begins. It occurs several times during this period, usually close to or sometimes on top of the nest box.

THE EGGS — The female may begin laying her eggs at any time once the nest has been completed, although she may wait up to a week. There is usually a lapse of at least a few days between completion of the nest and commencement of egg laying, with the pair remaining in the vicinity together. This coincides with the onset of the female's most fertile period, from a couple of days before the first egg of the clutch is laid until a couple of days before the last is laid. Each morning the female quietly deposits a single egg in the cup of the nest, until the clutch is complete. Recent studies have shown that all Eastern bluebirds lay their eggs at least one hour after sunrise, and that the median point for egg laying is around two hours after sunrise.[2]

2. Susan B. Meek and Raleigh J. Robertson, "Time of Day of Egg-Laying by Eastern Bluebirds," *Wilson Bulletin* 107, no. 2 (June 1995): pp. 377–79.

*The female removed most fecal sacs—
at first she'd go in and get them . . .*

*. . . later she'd remove
them from outside the box.*

*At the Pond Site the female brought
one item of food per visit . . .*

*. . . the male brought a number of
items all neatly tucked in his bill.*

*For most visits, the female
would land on top of the box.*

The male hardly ever did.

Typically, the clutch contains three to five, and occasionally six, clear blue eggs, each 21 × 16 mm (approximately $\frac{7}{8} \times \frac{5}{8}$"). The richness of the blue, a by-product of metabolism, may vary, and occasionally a female produces a clutch of white eggs. Not until all the eggs have been laid will the female begin incubating. This gives the young an equal chance for survival, as all eggs hatch at approximately the same time. It also makes the job of caring for the babies easier for the parents. It would be difficult to continue to incubate unhatched eggs with the added problem of finding food for hatchlings, and it is equally difficult to tend to fledglings while other birds remain in the nest. (Generally, incremental hatching seems totally inappropriate where clutch size is greater than two.) Occasionally, if an unusual warm spell occurs during the egg-laying time, and temperatures in the nest cavity are warm enough, embryonic development may occur without incubation, with the result that one or two eggs hatch before the others. With that in mind, one would have to wonder about the effect of almost certainly high temperatures on eggs of later broods. It seems likely that this situation would occur frequently, particularly when nest boxes are not well insulated from the sun (see Appendix II), and that the oldest and largest chick or chicks would receive the lion's share of the food at the expense of the others. However, additional help by young from the earlier brood, which is standard procedure, might help counteract any uneven distribution of food—with extra food being brought in, all chicks would still "get their fill."

By the start of May, egg laying had begun at all the nest sites I observed except the Road Site, where all aspects of the nesting cycle had begun earlier. All the nest boxes I observed, where I was able to make the determination, contained four eggs—the average for yearling females. In subsequent clutches, the number of eggs drops by one for each clutch; this includes older females whose first clutch might even have been more than four. However, a bluebird pair monitored by bluebird enthusiast Debbie Sheeley had five eggs in both their first and second clutch.

Toward the end of egg laying, the female—and only the female—forms a brood patch on her belly. When the feathers are parted, they reveal a warm, blood-engorged, reddish area of skin that increases warmth to the eggs by several degrees. And thus it is the female alone who incubates the eggs. Incubation is more or less an uninterrupted, twenty-four-hour-a-day job, including night, when the female sleeps on the nest. Although the male bluebird brings food to the female while she is incubating, she will leave occasionally—weather permitting—to do some of her own hunting. While she is away, the male may take her place on the nest, but this merely helps to conserve warmth for the eggs and is a stopgap measure. The female has a sense of how quickly she must return when the weather is cool and damp, but she feels free to stay away longer for hunting, drinking, and bathing during milder spells.

To keep her eggs evenly warmed, the female may turn them with her beak, particularly when she has just returned from one of her excursions out of the nest box. As the incubation period progresses and the embryos develop, her time on the nest becomes a more critical factor to the newborn chicks and her absences become fewer and more widely spaced. Typically, the eggs are incubated for thirteen or fourteen days, but adverse weather conditions, such as cold or rain, may slow development of the embryos and they may require up to an additional week before hatching.

FAMILY LIFE

THE HATCHLINGS — Baby bluebirds use a hard, temporary protuberance at the end of the beak, known as an egg tooth, to peck their way out of their shells. The process can take several hours, and the hatchlings arrive wet and tired. As soon as the eggs hatch, the female removes the bits of shell from the nest, eating some pieces for the calcium they contain and perhaps giving some to her mate, and then, so as not to alert predators to the chicks, she takes the remnants a considerable distance away from the nest to dispose of them.

The female stops at a
tree before flying to the box.

The male would
cling to a tree trunk . . .

Newly hatched bluebirds weigh less than one ounce, are blind and practically naked, and are in need of constant warmth. Their eyes are sealed shut. Sparse tufts of natal down are visible on their bright, coral-pink skin. The babies instinctively gape when a parent, uttering a greeting call, arrives at the entrance to the nest. They stretch their wobbly little necks and open wide to reveal their orange throats. Their peeping sounds stimulate the adults to feed them, and the orange of their throats guides the parents to the right spot in the darkness of the nesting cavity. In line with the "squeaky wheel" theory, the hungriest baby peeps the loudest and gapes the most—and food is

. . . or wait at the top of a small tree,

. . . then fly in,

given to that chick first. When each in turn is satisfied, it quiets down. Thus all chicks are fed.

The babies' excrement is encased in a thin membrane called a fecal sac. The sacs are easily and promptly removed, disposed of by the parents far enough away so as not to leave predator-attracting scents near the nest cavity. At the Pond Site, where I was able to get the best view of exactly what went in and out, these sacs were removed after each feeding after a consecutive number of visits, so that I was able to estimate the number of young in the nest based on the number of fecal sacs consecutively removed. At the Pond Site, that number was four. The female removed most of the sacs; only occasionally did the male take one out.

The baby birds grow rapidly, and within the first couple of days their skin takes on a bluish cast as feathers begin forming beneath it. By the time the nestlings are one week old, their eyes have begun to open and their first feathers burst from the tips of sheaths. Although she may leave the nest to eat, drink, or bathe during warm, sunny days, up to this time the mother almost constantly broods the young, including overnight, as they are unable to generate their own heat to keep warm.

During that first week, the male feeds both the babies and the mother. However, once the babies' feathers begin to emerge, brooding ceases and the female joins the male full time in the feeding. Within another half-week, the babies' eyes will be fully opened and their sex can be determined: wing and tail feathers are a deeper cobalt blue on the males, duller on females, and the females show white edging on their outer tail feathers. Raising the young is an arduous task indeed, requiring strenuous and energetic nonstop labor from sunrise to sunset. Small, soft-shelled insects are the first foods given to the hatchlings, brought to the nest at roughly five-minute intervals throughout the day by both parents (and later also by the young bluebirds from earlier broods). Thus, in a brood of four young, each individual is fed approximately once every twenty minutes.

CARING FOR THE NESTLINGS — At the Garden Site, the parents made approximately an equal number of visits to the nest box to feed their babies, with each appearing to carry one bit of food per visit. They would go directly to the box, cling to its outside for a second or two, and then either go all the way inside, as when the chicks were young, or stick only their heads inside the box. The situation at the Road Site was just about the same. At the Pond Site, however, the female made many more trips than the male; but for each visit, the male would bring back a number of items—an ant, a caterpillar, and a dragonfly, for instance—all neatly tucked into his beak. Here, they brought food just about continuously for fifteen minutes and then rested for the next fifteen minutes. For most visits, the female would land on top of the

. . . hang on,

. . . and make the delivery.

*The male would reach in just far
enough to deposit food in the gaping
little mouths . . .*

*. . . or else
pass it over to Mama
for distribution.*

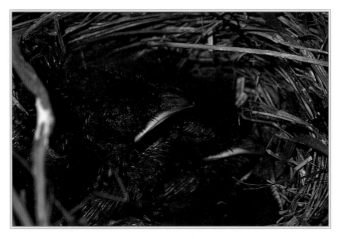

The nest at the Pond Site contained four chicks.

*A nestling
gaping at the nest hole.*

*A little head
juts out to meet its parent.*

box first, whereas the male hardly ever did. He, instead, would cling to the bark of a tree trunk or wait at the top of a small tree or shrub until the female had departed. Then he would fly in, hang on, and make the delivery.

In the beginning, when the Pond Site nestlings were very young, both parents took food into the nest box. Later, while the female was still entering the box, the male would hang on to the outside of the box or the edge of the opening, and he would dip his head in just far enough to reach and deposit food in the gaping mouths, or he would pass it to Mama for distribution to the chicks. At this site, the male entered the nest box only very infrequently and even less frequently did he come out with a fecal sac. From what I was able to determine, he did not engage in any housekeeping. Just about every time the female went inside, however, she stayed longer than he would. I could hear the babies' muffled, begging peeps, as well as faint vocalizations that sounded similar to a dove's *coo* and some noise similar to the pecking of a woodpecker, as—I presume—Mama cleaned the nest.

When the nestlings were about ten days old, Don Sweeney, the bluebird advocate who led me to the lovely Pond Site, checked the nest box for bluebird blowfly larvae (see Appendix II for information regarding blowfly infestation). He removed the nest, then plucked out and discarded approximately ten larvae—a mild infestation for a first brood (infestations tend to get heavier and be more troublesome with subsequent broods). If the infestation had been a heavy one, Don would have fashioned a new nest out of dry grasses and discarded the old. As I had expected, the nest contained four chicks, but one chick was smaller than the rest.

At this point, an explosion of growth was occurring inside the nest box. By the time the nestlings were eleven days old, they gaped at the nest hole when they heard their parents' voices. By the next day, a little head jutted out to meet its parent for some food. By that time, feeding was nonstop, without the rest periods the parents had enjoyed earlier.

At two weeks old, the young had become quite active and were almost ready for their maiden flights. A bluebird's first flight occurs some time during its third week.

OUT OF THE NEST — When weather conditions are optimum for the nestlings—calm and warm, with food abundant—the young may be ready to leave the nest in as little as two weeks. Conversely, cool, damp conditions with correspondingly low insect availability may keep them nestbound for three weeks. Midway between the two—seventeen to eighteen days—is average.

Toward the end of the nestling stage, the young become quite active, moving around, probably climbing on top of one another, exercising their wings, stretching, and preening. Both parents and young know instinctively that it is time. The parents stop bringing food to the nest, offering it instead from a nearby perch. They become noisy and active around the nest, coaxing the young and encouraging them to leave the box. One after the other, the nestlings climb to the opening, look around, and propel themselves up to one hundred feet away, to the nearest perch—a shrub, a fence, or a small tree. Although flights and landings must still be perfected, the parents do not need to teach the young to fly   it is instinctive.

After that short maiden flight, the young—now called fledglings—work their way to the upper branches of the trees, where they instinctively huddle together for warmth and safety. They now give a sad little call to their parents to announce their location and ask for food. Both parents continue to feed the fledglings, unless the female has begun construction of a new nest in preparation for her next brood. In that case, the male feeds and protects the babies.

By the second week, the fledglings begin to follow their parents around the neighborhood, and within three weeks they begin to do some of their own foraging. To get the knack of hunting, they may pick up insects on branches or the ground, for as youngsters they seem to peck at everything, but within another week the fledglings hunt in typical bluebird fashion, dropping down on an insect spotted from a perch.

By the time the young have been out of the nest for about one month, the parents gradually stop feeding them and the young become more self-sufficient. In another week or so, the young—now called juveniles—are on their own.

Juvenile bluebirds usually remain with their parents throughout the breeding season, and they frequently are enlisted as helpers with subsequent broods. Occasionally, siblings from a previous season may also pitch in—a real family effort. As we shall see in the next chapter, the act of feeding is not necessarily a behavior that is learned through imitation, appearing instead to be an inborn desire. Possibly the part of feeding that *is* learned through imitation is using the nest box opening for delivery of food to the nestlings.

With help from juveniles of earlier broods, the nestling phase may be shortened. This is desirable, in that the longer the nestlings stay in the nest, the more prone the clutch is to blowfly infestation and the greater the chance of overheating in the nest box. When the parents have helpers, they complete the nesting chores sooner and more safely, making a third brood possible in many areas. Thus, the parents are able to raise more young and the young, rather than being banished from the parents' territory, are welcomed. As part of the family effort, the young benefit by learning the skills they will need when they become parents, and they have the added advantage and protection of group life.

BONNIE AND BEN

Superbly cared for by their devoted parents, the young bluebirds at the Pond Site grew stronger every day, and it was getting near the time for them to leave the nest box. They might fledge any day now and I didn't want to miss it. I wanted to have my camera ready for that moment when a fluffy little bluebird climbs to the exit, looks up at the trees, and catapults toward the next chapter in its life.

On June 4, I arrived bright and early to monitor the nest box. The threat of severe thunderstorms had stopped me from going out the day before, and I was

paticularly anxious to see what progress had occurred.
When I arrived, I noticed the male immediately as he
flew from the ground to the canopy of tall trees. "Oh
good," I thought, "they're still here." I set up my camera
equipment and sat under the camouflage netting. I
waited for one of the parents to appear at the box with
some tasty morsel to feed one of the babies or to coax it
out of the box. But something was wrong—everything
was quiet and there were no trips to the box. Again, however, the male appeared in the vicinity, caught something
on the ground, and flew back to the treetops. Apparently
the nestlings had fledged either that morning or, perhaps, the day before. I scanned the area repeatedly with
binoculars, hoping to catch a glimpse of one of them
being fed by a parent. But I saw nothing and heard nothing—no calling, no begging. Still, the male made an
appearance every once in a while and then returned
almost immediately to the treetops. The fledglings
should be in close proximity to one another, but he,
strangely, was not returning to the same place each time.
Though I heard no calls, I took that as an indication that
they had just fledged and had not yet coordinated their
locations.

FOSTER BABIES—ORPHANED AND ABANDONED

Somewhat disappointed in having missed the maiden
flights, and now unable to determine where the young had

been secreted, I packed up my equipment and placed it in the car. Just as I was ready to leave, I recalled that one chick was smaller than the rest, and I hoped that it had been strong enough to accompany the others. My conscience wouldn't allow me to leave without being sure. So I put my ear against the side of the box and listened . . . dead silence. That in and of itself is not so unusual—noise is a dead giveaway to predators, and babies tend to be relatively quiet until a parent arrives to feed them. Next, I took a little round mirror on a long handle from my camera bag, a dentist's type mirror. I attempted to look in the box through the hole, but couldn't see anything. Still, I wasn't satisfied. Although I couldn't see anything, I was unable to be sure that it hadn't been left behind. The box would have to be opened.

I searched for something to loosen the screw on the nest box and eventually decided on the butt end of a nail file. I lifted the front door, fully expecting to see the customary trampled-down, soiled, and empty nest, but instead I saw a little head burrowed down among the dried grass. A baby bluebird, alive but just as quiet as could be. I immediately closed the nest box and moved a considerable distance away to observe. I began to worry —it had been at least forty-five minutes since I had arrived and the bird had not been fed even once during that time. I moved as far away as possible and watched for any sign of activity. I saw the male occasionally, but each time he retreated to the treetops; the female was not to be seen at all, and I speculated that she was tending to the babies—or might even be starting a new nest for another brood.

Four hours is the rule of thumb. When there has been no activity observed at a nest box for that long, one may consider the occupants either orphaned or abandoned, as the case may be. I wanted neither to disturb the nest nor discourage either parent from returning; but after at least five and one-half hours something had to be done. I had only waited that long because the male *had* been seen. Nestlings are fed on the average of once every fifteen to twenty minutes. This nestling had been more than five hours without food. I tossed the matter around and around in my mind. Should I try to find something to feed it? And then what—wait another five and one-half hours? Should I take it home?

The best place for the bird, of course, is with its own kind, as it would come to know the ways of the bluebird that are learned instead of just inherited. That is the ideal situation; but if I were to intervene, the bird would *have* to be removed. I got out the nail file again and reopened the box. A little female sat there, cool and listless. She didn't gape for food and made no begging noises. All lingering doubts about taking action left my mind. I took a cotton fisherman's hat from my car, lined the inside with dry grasses, and made an indentation to simulate the real nest cup. It would be the perfect way to transport her. Then, when I reached in to lift her out, I noticed another baby, considerably smaller, right behind her. With the beautiful cobalt blue so noticeable on the wings, I could tell it was a male. For some reason, I felt less guilty removing two than one. Actually, it was a blessing: the little brother and sister could retain their genetic identity and interact with one another in a bluebird way. It would make the job easier when they would ultimately be released.

There were no signs of disturbance in the nest box, with no loose feathers or blood around and no claw marks on the post. Accordingly, I ruled out predation by a cat or raccoon. If a raccoon had gotten to the nest, it is most certain that all four chicks would have been taken, the nest would have been pulled out at least partially, and there would be feathers around. But a snake would not leave such a trail, and so that was a possibility. A bluebird parent might easily forsake a nest if he or she were to see a snake in it, and that could account for the disappearance of two babies and the apparent abandonment of the others. But where was the female? Since she was not observed at all, and the male was catching insects at ground level and moving into the treetops, I had to

The Babies were hand-warmed.

When we hit the right "bluebird note," the Babies gaped.

presume that he was feeding someone, presumably the two who had fledged.

Perhaps these two nestlings were not ready to fledge. It was surprising not to see at least one parent continuing to care for the nestlings or, at the very least, attempting to coax them out. My rationale was that they had made the choice to care for the two nestlings sure to survive. As it turned out, the body of the female was later discovered on the opposite side of the pond from where the nest box was situated. There were no marks on her and how she met her demise is unknown. But that discovery did much to explain the lack of attention to the babies in the box. The widowed parent could not tend to babies at two different levels in two different locations. He *had* to make a choice, and obviously he elected to abandon the weaker two in favor of the ones more likely to reach adulthood.

A BIGGER NEST

I brought home the pair, about fifteen days old, cradled among the grasses in the upturned hat. They were cool and quiet, and showed none of the expected signs of hunger. While my husband went out to get some fresh mealworms for them, my mother and I warmed the babies in our hands. It is senseless to attempt to feed a cool chick —it needs to be warmed up first. Once the food arrived, I picked up a mealworm with dull tweezers to simulate a beak and attempted to get them to open their mouths. I whistled, I tapped, I tried swooping down from above with the food. I whistled while touching the top and sides of their beaks, and I stroked their backs (although this certainly worked well later), all to no avail. All of a sudden my mother, whistling along with me, hit just the right "bluebird note" and both mouths popped open in unison.

Until bluebird fledglings are totally self-sufficient, they receive food supplements from the parents—frequently from the male since the female may be on the way to her next brood. So for these babies in my care I was going to have to work out some method of supplying food and later supplementing their diets. The *only* way would be for them to come to me for food. I would have to try to reverse something instinctive in them. I started out by placing the birds in my hand or on one of my fingers to be fed, and I whistled and called, "Babies." Eventually, I hoped, when I would whistle and call, they would come to my hand on their own. That first day they had little strength to lift their bodies above their legs, and they wobbled when I tried to get them to cling to and perch on my finger to be fed—they were just too weak.

To keep them safe and warm between feedings and overnight, I placed the babies in a grass-lined nest in a spare bluebird nest box and put the box in the sunroom. When placed in the box, they promptly retired to separate corners.

When placed in the box, they retired to separate corners.

Their wing feathers had almost grown in and the tail feathers had a good start.

The Babies looked like little balls of fluff.

Mad at the world.

It is frequently noted that, when nest boxes are monitored for blowfly larvae, if nestlings are removed from the nest after the twelfth or thirteenth day, they may bolt when replaced, fledging prematurely when they would be unable to care for themselves. I kept the babies in the nest box for the first days and removed them only for feeding and some exercise. Contrary to expectation, however, they stayed exactly where I put them, with no fussing. Of course, it may have been that they did not relate the round opening to an escape route, as no one entered that way to feed them and they were removed and replaced via the side door.

Taking my clues from nature, I fed them at fifteen- to twenty-minute intervals. Searching for food among the grasses, as bluebird parents do, proved to be an exercise in futility, as I couldn't possibly keep up with their needs. I developed a genuine appreciation for the diligence, devotion, and abilities of bluebird parents. In addition to mealworms, I purchased small crickets and, to offer even more variety, dug earthworms from the garden—at four-thirty in the morning. This would be a big job, and very time-consuming, but the Babies were adorable and worth every minute.

Although the wing feathers had almost grown in and the tail feathers had a good start on their way to attaining full length, the birds were still sparsely covered with tufts of down and looked like little balls of fluff. The down appeared above and behind each eye, looking quite like little horns. This, coupled with their too-wide-for-their-faces, downturned, yellow beaks, made them appear as though they were mad at the world. Once they were given a couple of meals, however, they began their miraculous recovery, with little shows of strength here and there. By the following day, they were able to lift their little bodies off their feet and exercise their wings—the latter mostly accomplished while standing on the other's head. It is interesting to note that by the second day, the Babies' excrement was no longer encased in a fecal sac.

It certainly made no difference to them, but I had to endow them with names. She became Bonnie for Bonnie Blue Butler of *Gone with the Wind*, and he became Ben, for Ben Blue.

To add even more to what had become a mystery, within four days of the "fledging," the male at the Pond Site was observed to spend the day singing his heart out and later was seen with a new female, investigating nest boxes. The plan was to release the Babies in due time to their birth area, in hope and anticipation that they might rejoin their biological family. But under the circumstances, with no family to hook up with, I decided it might be just as well—or even better—to release them where I might monitor and protect them.

Ben climbs on Bonnie's head and exercises his wings.

By the third day the Babies were allowed to remain in the Ficus.

Ben, pushing off his perch, takes dead aim for my head.

FLIGHT — By their second day here, the Babies were taking short flights—from my hand to the back of the love seat, from the love seat to my head—but it is likely that they could have gone much farther under normal circumstances. They seemed to enjoy landing on my head, perhaps because it is my highest point. Each time they were ready—and they did most things in unison—they would crouch down, perhaps bob up and down once or twice, and crouch again as if trying to gain or start momentum, and then spring off the perch. I reasoned it would be appropriate to have some branches—with leaves—for practicing flights and landings. A large *Ficus* borrowed from my mother was placed in the corner of the sunroom. I expected this to be home base. But no sooner did I place them in the tree than Ben climbed up to the top of her head and exercised his wings.

By their third day, instead of returning them to the nest box between feedings, I placed them on a branch of the *Ficus* tree. There they would sit and preen—obviously instinctive behavior—and then rest. By their fourth day, I no longer returned them to the nest box at all and their flying skills improved. Now, instead of the *Ficus*, they would spend all their spare time sitting on the blades of the ceiling fan. It was a comical sight, indeed. Each time one would move, the fan would rotate a tad and they would have to hop from one blade to the next to stay in the position, relative to the sunroom itself, where they wanted to be. Of course, the more they moved, the more the fan moved, too.

As was to be expected, their flying abilities improved daily. By the time they had been with me a week and were three weeks old, their flights were just about perfect —taking into account the constraints of the sunroom.

FOOD — It didn't take long for the Babies to recognize me, and their eyes would follow me around the room after just the first few feedings. Their excitement at the prospect of being fed was evident. Baby bluebirds know their parents first by sound and then by sight, since their eyes are sealed shut at birth. But the Babies seemed to know me first by sight and later they would become excited just hearing my voice. Before long, when they were hungry and saw me, they'd stretch and flutter their wings, chirp, bob up and down, go through the feeding motions with one another, and flutter and chirp some more—they were begging.

Despite the fact that they had already attained most of their adult weight, during the first week Ben and Bonnie appeared to grow by leaps and bounds, seeming larger each time they were fed. To sustain such a rapid growth and ongoing changes, they had voracious appetites and consumed copious quantities of food. At three weeks of age, the fledglings should be released. I could not do that, however, until they were able to obtain enough food to survive, whether totally self-sufficient or partially self-sufficient and coming to me for supplements.

It was very difficult not to bring something to them when they begged, but as long as I continued to give in to them, they'd never learn. Ben caught on quickly to the concept of feeding reversal and came over to be fed regularly. Bonnie, however, was adamant about food being brought to her, and she would quiver her wings and chatter to me, insisting that I comply. She was a stubborn little female and needed much coaxing. Ben was the smallest of the clutch, and it is possible that he was forced to be the most resourceful—or not eat. Also, I must admit, I didn't make teaching her any easier, as I would feel sorry for her and then usually give in after a time.

The Babies being hand-fed.

I always took them away from where they were sitting
to be fed—at least for daytime feedings. So even when I
did give in to Bonnie, I brought her to where Ben had
been fed. At first Ben would only fly to me when he was
"famished." He would bob up and down, push off the
perch, and take dead aim for the top of my head. I would
then nudge him onto my finger and bring him around to
the front of me. Before long, it became automatic with
him. This, I believe, was because I always offered an
attractive cricket first. As it became more automatic with
Ben, Bonnie began to mimic his actions. Eventually we
were on the right path, but I would still have to introduce
them to the concept of picking up food on their own.

Within days, as they would under natural fledging circumstances, the Babies started to peck at leaves and
branches on the *Ficus*, at one another's feet, at the mealworms at the end of the tweezers, at the crickets. Each
step one took, the other independently took as well—
almost as though there is a genetic schedule at play.
Pecking, especially when they began pecking at and
pulling the loose, thin quilting threads on the love seat's
cover (similar to a robin tugging at an earthworm), indicated to me that they might be ready to start picking up
some of their own food. This would be another hurdle to
cross while they were being readied for release.

Eventually the time came, as I suspected it would,
when Bonnie took some initiative about coming over for

food. On her tenth day, she took half a cricket from the
tweezers. Since I was sure that it wasn't able to jump
away, I dropped the other half to see if she would pick it
up, and she did. About the same time that Bonnie became
more aggressive about food, Ben flew down off his fan
perch and, instead of landing on my head only to be
brought down to hand level, he landed on the hand
holding the tweezers and proceeded to take the cricket
from the tweezers himself by pulling it apart and snatching pieces. That was the first time he had taken food
without having it come from overhead. Ben was growing
up, and I knew that within a couple of days the Babies
would be ready to be released. The dangers associated
with the early fledgling period were quickly waning, and
it would be much safer for them outdoors.

Although mealworms are easy to catch and handle,
and they are chock-full of protein, it seemed appropriate
to vary the bluebirds' diet, offering other critters as well.
In the beginning, extra concentration was placed either
on the soft, whitish mealworm just after it sheds its chiti-
nous shell or on earthworms, each because of its softness
and expected digestibility. Later more emphasis was
placed on crickets, since this is a favored natural food
and one offered by parents. In addition, the crickets
produced the most desirable response of exciting the
birds, even from a distance. Other little garden treasures
were given to them as well, but as I was unsure of the

I preferred that they sleep in the Ficus.

They became one ball of fluff.

Each morning their heads would be tucked back, facing in opposite directions.

benefit of many of the items, that practice was kept to a minimum.

Much controversy surrounds the offering of peanut butter to birds, with some folks claiming that it sticks in the birds' mouths and soils their feathers. Some feel that it does no harm. That aside, I believe everyone will agree that the fats and proteins available in peanut butter make it a valuable additive to the diet, especially in winter. The mix that I offered the birds (see Appendix III for recipe) is very granular or mealy. The birds love it and for years they have been using it to feed their own rapidly growing, demanding babies. Robins and mockingbirds bring their babies and feed it to them, mouthful after mouthful, as do bluejays, chickadees, and titmice. The red-bellied woodpeckers and cardinals pick up chunks and take them back to their nests. And those little insectivores, the downy and hairy woodpeckers, position their babies about eight feet away and carry pieces to them. The orioles won't leave it alone, preferring it to both apples and oranges, and the din of young starlings is deafening during their fledgling period, when the parents bring them to the mix.

The peanut butter mix is compatible with bluebirds' needs, too. Bluebirds will use feeders properly constructed and stocked with something they like and want, and this mixture could provide adequately for them, should they spend the winter. The mixture in tandem with berries of dogwood, sumac, holly, or Virginia creeper could make the difference between a successful winter and a failed one. So, while the Babies were perfecting their skills—that is, going to the food as opposed to the food coming to them—it seemed appropriate to introduce them to the mix as well. They ate the little bits that were offered, but seemed somewhat confused at first by the consistency and definitely preferred the live stuff.

SLEEP — When it was time to go to sleep, the Babies preferred to roost at the highest spot, either a blade of the fan or, later, the space between the fan's motor and the ceiling. I preferred that they sleep in the *Ficus*. I felt a "tree" is more natural, but primarily the smooth surfaces of the fan parts gave them nothing to clasp with their feet. So, I moved them to a branch on the tree and they settled in, moving sideways on the branch until the two individuals became one ball of fluff, cuddle, and talk. But the minute I left the room, they returned to the fan. Once it became dark enough, however, they would stay where I put them. All during twilight, Bonnie and Ben would warble and clasp beaks. It took a long time before silence would fall over the *Ficus*, but each morning their heads would be tucked back, facing in opposite directions.

BATH — Bluebirds delight in bathwater. They flutter their wings and tails, thoroughly immersing themselves, including the head. This, I've read, is not an instinctive behavior but an activity that must be learned through trial and error or imitation.

When the Babies were approximately three weeks old, I began to think about the activities that they needed to learn—bathing, hunting, singing. Until proficient in coming to me for food, they would be housebound, and that time could be put to good use. Surely I couldn't teach them to sing, and I had already begun to work on hunting—that left bathing.

I placed a terra-cotta saucer about two inches deep on a stool in the middle of the sunroom, and I filled it to about one inch with water comfortable to the touch. Although the little copycats had been pretty much equal

Bluebirds delight in bathwater—here Bonnie and Ben inspect the bath.

A good way not to get wet.

Splashing.

Ben takes a dunk.

in most aspects of learning, Ben had exhibited much more leadership when learning to come to me for food and, therefore, he seemed the most likely candidate to first know about a bath. I hoped Bonnie would imitate him.

I picked Ben up and placed him in the middle of the bath. His tail got wet, but he left the water within seconds, not allowing any of it to touch his other feathers. Perhaps they weren't ready for that yet. Nevertheless, Bonnie, too, should at least have a taste of what was being offered. As with Ben, I picked Bonnie up and placed her in the center of the saucer, but this time I swished the water around a bit with my finger. To my surprise, she fluttered her wings and shook her tail. She did that three or four times, and then lowered her head and dunked it in the water, fluttered and splashed a little more, and dunked her head again. There was no need to teach her anything; bathing came quite naturally. Afterward, she dried off by shaking and then hunching her shoulders and wings forward, keeping her wings straight down with feathers spread. Then she preened. The following day, Ben also took a bath, and from then on, they took one together—just another place to play.

A LOVING BOND

Bonnie and Ben wanted to be near one another all the time. They would move as close as possible to each other, but no matter how close that was, they never seemed satisfied that it was close enough. The move to get closer might be initiated by either one, but it was usually initiated by Ben. In fact, they huddled most of the time, but particularly as sunset approached. And, of course, they slept that way, too. If one would move away a bit, the other would gape, almost in a threatening, reprimanding manner, and then move sideways along the branch until the two individuals became one ball of fluff again. All day long they'd softly warble to one another, almost chattering; they'd clasp beaks and pretend to feed one another; and when they were placed in the tree for the night, I could hear their soft, whispered conversation well into twilight. What does it mean? Are they quietly relating their positions or whereabouts to parents or siblings? Why, then, would they do that at other times—for instance, when he snuggled under my chin? Their constant billing and cooing reminded me of lovebirds.

Their favorite place to be was on the fan blades, but of course neither wanted to be there alone. After Ben would leave the sleeping branch in the morning for a cricket breakfast, he would fly up to the fan and call his sister. If she failed to follow, he would return to the tree, make his way back to her, and then wait until she was ready to get up, too. This would be a precursor to his later behavior—for it would be Bonnie, always, who would call the shots.

Drying off on my camera equipment.

Bonnie reprimands Ben for not being close enough.

Their favorite place was the fan blades.

Bonnie flew to the catalpa.

Togetherness undoubtedly serves to protect the young birds in the wild by keeping them in one place so the parents might easily tend to them. Thus, this huddling behavior serves a purpose. Nevertheless, it is truly one of the most endearing aspects of their nature, and nothing else that they did captured my heart the way this intimate behavior had.

There was such a loving bond between them that each time I would see them being affectionate—hear them call to one another or otherwise lovingly interact—I would feel thankful that there had been two babies in that box and not just one. I can think of nothing truly sadder than a bluebird growing up alone. But the best part was their gentle, loving ways and cozy moments extended to me as well, for I was accepted as one of them and included in their circle of intimacy and affection. Warbling seemed to be the breakthrough, for when I would warble in a soft, albeit primitive, way, Ben would alight on my chest and hop up and snuggle under my chin, stare at me, and open and close his beak the way he would with his sister. He enjoyed flying to my shoulder and pecking at my t-shirt and pulling loose strands of my hair. On several occasions, he even attempted to nibble at either my eye or eyelashes.

GRADUATION

As mentioned earlier, fledging occurs roughly at two and one-half weeks. The fledgling period is probably the most dangerous time in the life of a bluebird, and the first twenty-four hours are the most critical. It is then that they are most vulnerable, not fast or agile enough, not self-sufficient, and not yet having learned much about bluebird life. For a week after fledging, the babies remain hidden and continue to be fed and protected by the parents. By the time the youngsters are one month old, they begin hunting, and it is another one to two weeks before they may be considered self-sufficient.

Theoretically, by the time Bonnie and Ben were released these birds would have fledged in the conventional way. They may have successfully made their way to the treetops and huddled together, warbling to one another and pecking at everything in sight, including one another's feet, while they waited for food. But that time for Ben and Bonnie instead was spent in the sunroom. There they learned to come to me for food and perfected their flying and landing skills. When they willingly picked up their own food and showed signs that they wanted to catch some as well, they were ready. They had bypassed the most potentially dangerous period of their lives unscathed, but they were ready to graduate and start another new chapter.

I was sure that they would come to me for food. They had been responsive to my voice and knew me by sight as well. Sunday afternoon, June 18—just two weeks after they had arrived—I called them from outside the

Together in the weeping cherry.

*The Babies came to the
latticework just outside the sunroom.
Ben . . .*

Bonnie . . .

. . . the Babies.

sunroom for a tidbit. Ben flew to my shoulder and Bonnie
to my hand, and each took what was offered. They
looked around at the trees and everything else in the
new, wide world around them. But when I tried walking
them out farther away from the house, Ben flew back to
the top of the screen door that had been left ajar, Bonnie
to the railing. In unison, they flew back indoors to the
safety of the fan blade. From the nest box to the sunroom, from the sunroom to this—it had proved momen-
tarily to be too much. But we tried again, and this time
Ben flew to the chokecherry and, within seconds, Bonnie
flew to the catalpa. They did very well: both the flights
and the landings were nearly perfect, but they weren't

together. My husband saw Ben fly to the tallest trees in the garden, the sassafras trees, but Bonnie was nowhere to be found.

I called "Babies," and whistled. They returned my call. Their call is not a very robust one. In fact, it's a mild, almost meek, somewhat sad little two-syllable call, but it was discernible to me over all the others in the garden, and it was music to my ears. But they didn't leave the treetops. We called back and forth for over an hour. "How could I have been so wrong," I thought. I kept trying. I called, they answered. Finally the two were spotted together in a sassafras tree. Then Bonnie flew back to the catalpa and then to the weeping cherry, and Ben followed. I sat in the middle of the lawn and held up a cricket in the tweezers, in an attempt to entice them when, all of a sudden, Ben flew by. He wanted to land on my head in his usual manner, but he stopped. Something was different: there was no love seat behind me. After two or three attempts, Ben made it and began eating. When he was finished, he flew again to the catalpa and joined Bonnie. To get her to eat, I had to coax her, branch by branch, down to a spot where I could just about reach her, and meet her halfway. After that, the pair came to where I would sit just outside the sunroom on a regular basis whenever they were called, more frequently if they were hungry.

The first habit that the Babies formed was "coming in for the landing." Invariably, it was on an angled drainpipe off the sunroom. "Boom," as they plunked down announced their presence. At times, unable to maintain a grip, they would slide off. In short order, it became automatic that they return to the drainpipe each time before coming down to eat. They would play on the drainpipe, and most times when they landed on it, they would spread their wings and tails, turn their heads to face the sun, and soak up some solar power—regardless of the amount of heat—for a couple of minutes before begging for food. Soaking up the sun's rays in such a fashion was a very regular activity, and oblivious to danger, they seemed to do it anytime and anyplace, whether on the drain, in the grass, or on top of some latticework.

This is a critical time in the life of baby birds, a time when one can witness cardinal or robin parents—as well as a host of others—literally spending hours coaching their young and coaxing them into hiding as each new danger appears. Bonnie and Ben were on their own, with no one to guard them in the treetops. The ground, however, was another story, and I would stay with them and watch over them constantly until they became self-sufficient.

As days passed, the babies were fed at regular intervals of approximately thirty to forty minutes, and they were

Ben spreads his wings and tail . . .

. . . and soaks in some sun.

They often napped on the latticework . . .

. . . at other times, on the branch of a tree.

allowed to eat until satisfied. A meal might contain only two crickets each, or it could have as much as three or four crickets and six to eight mealworms each. Whatever it was, even their appetites were in sync. They always arrived together and always seemed satisfied with equal portions of food, more or less.

The Babies napped frequently in between feedings—right down to drawing the nictitating membranes up over the eyes—often on the latticework right behind the sunroom, at other times on a branch of a tree. Most often they would face opposite one another on the branch during their repose, and I had to wonder if that is instinctive, enabling them as a unit to monitor all directions for danger.

Preparing for their afternoon siesta, they would push and shove one another on the branch as they attempted to find the most comfortable spot, just as two little children vying for the best spot on the couch might do. Occasionally they would inadvertently separate and wind up in different trees from one another. When that happened, they'd call back and forth, never losing contact with one another until they would reunite. But I noticed that Bonnie usually called and Ben dropped whatever he was doing to fly to her. He always catered to her, and if they had been separated for a while, he'd act so excited—even relieved—when they met again, whereas she'd be cool and undaunted. As they got older, that would happen more often, and they would look for one another at home base or go to the weeping cherry tree and call from out in the open. They were kindred spirits, these two. If one would bathe, the other would join in; if one napped, so did the other. They cuddled together, chattered, and warbled, just like two little peas in a pod. Their bond continued.

Bonnie and Ben inspected everything, and much time was involved in pecking at branches in the spruce tree, presumably for the ants that they loved so much. Even more time was spent on the porch overhang. They pecked, tugged, and pulled at every pine needle, dried-up leaf or other airborne debris to have landed in the gutters as they looked for ants and spiders or other arthropods—or whatever it is that bluebirds look for. I would sit and watch one pine needle after another being passed through their bills, bite by bite, or back and forth to one another and then dropped to the ground below. Frequently they'd take mealworms up there as well.

They really seemed to enjoy the gutter. Often they would sit in it, using the gutter as a vantage point from which to monitor the surroundings below—their little heads would pop up and they would silently look over and down at anyone who walked by beneath them. They would peck and scavenge, and climb back and forth over one another while in the gutter. Bluebirds are inquisitive creatures with an inclination to investigate every little

The Babies pecked at everything—here Ben explores the latticework.

Mealworms were placed in a tray for the Babies.

Bonnie and Ben picked up every-thing—here it is a spruce cone . . .

. . . a stick,

. . . a dried-up blade of grass.

Bluebirds' wings seem relatively large.

crack, crevice, or opening. On numerous occasions, Ben
would push his beak in between my fingers at the base,
investigating the little space between them. The gutters
were just another little cavity to investigate.

The Babies answered my morning calls, but they would
roost long after other birds stopped singing from their
roosting perches. Some birds are early risers—humming-
birds, robins, and cardinals are active at the crack of dawn
—but apparently bluebirds like to sleep in a bit longer. At
least Bonnie and Ben did. When they were in the sunroom
they'd wake up but remain perched at the roosting spot,
warbling to one another, pecking, or just looking around.
That didn't change very much once they were released.
While woodpeckers, bluejays, finches, and sparrows
would be active at the feeders, Bonnie and Ben were still
just calling back and forth to me and probably warbling to
one another, pecking, or just looking around.

When we were making the transition to picking up
their own food, I would place mealworms in a pile on the
ground or on a tray for them to pick up on their own, but
still used the tweezers for crickets, which they wanted
head-first and down. At times they wouldn't even take
them unless they were in that position. If a cricket's feel-
ers were too long, they—especially Ben—would pull
them off or just look at them until I repositioned it. By
Day Three outdoors, each time they'd make a feeding

visit, they'd forage around on the ground for food of their own as well. Since they now were spending time foraging on the ground behind the house, and there is always the danger of a stealthy cat, I thought it wise to make some provisions for their safety. I installed a window-box holder on the deck railing and inserted a plastic window box in it. I could then line the bottom with several dozen meal-worms and the Babies could help themselves. The pan was deep enough and smooth-sided to confine the ever-moving mealworms while keeping the birds off the ground and away from ground predators. The pan was easily visi-ble from the spruce tree where they liked to sit and was attractively located—they could just hop right in and take what they wanted. Bonnie was more aggressive in this regard than Ben, a typical little female asserting her inde-pendence from the start, visiting the pan within minutes of its installation. Ben preferred to stay on the ground, but would follow Bonnie in there from time to time.

Bonnie was an aggressive hunter in many regards. She'd pick up any object not too heavy—pieces of paper and leaves three times her size or long sticks. I presumed that she looked under them for critters. Ben did that too, but Bonnie enjoyed it more. One day she caught herself a daddy long legs but I think the legs confused or both-ered her. She put it down and picked it up repeatedly, as though she were looking for an answer about how to just

Ben talks to me.

Ben after a bath,

. . . drying off in the sun.

Ben would land gracefully on the hummingbird perch.

eat the middle. Then she put it down and picked up a small woody stem about two inches long and began smacking it down in a swishing motion, first to one side then the other, in the vicinity of her dropped prey. What does that mean? What *could* it mean? Dare I entertain the possibility that she is capable of using a tool?

It was appropriate to encourage such grownup behavior as hunting, so when Bonnie would hop around, hunting among the pine needle mulch, I would drop a cricket for her to find on her own. The crickets were quick, but Bonnie was quicker and she'd catch them each and every time. When a cricket would drop from her beak to the ground, she'd recatch it in a heartbeat. She was good, but Ben, although he would forage, was rather content to fly over and land on my arm, head, hand, or shoulder and allow me to feed him. In rather typical female fashion, Bonnie was very friendly, but aloof. Ben was more lovable —he still gazed into my eyes while warbling to me and was comfortable enough to sit and relax on my finger or fall fast asleep in my cupped hand for ten or fifteen minutes.

Bonnie and Ben, with their gentle, loving personalities, were as cute and endearing as they could possibly be, but no matter how cute they may be, they still look like little predators—large eyes, hawk-type beaks, swallow-type shoulders, and streamlined bodies. I don't know what the wing size is in relation to the body—nor do I know how that measurement would compare with other birds, but to me their wings seemed to be relatively large. They easily reminded me of falcons.

What did the Babies do all day? They ate, took siestas, "talked," snoozed, played in the gutter, occasionally bathed, and played, played, played. In spite of not having anyone to "show them the ropes," the Babies progressed rapidly and changes were evident even after just one week outdoors. But all too soon they stopped being babyish. Instead of landing on me or the drainpipe, Ben would gracefully land on the hummingbird perch near the spruce tree. Bonnie would, too, but she never stopped landing on the hand with the tweezers. She liked to do that. Now, when they would alight on the clothesline, they'd perch normally instead of rocking back and forth.

Even though they still seemed to enjoy being hand-fed, or at least were not ready to give up that security entirely, that was changing, too. They seemed to prefer that I just pass an offering to them, tweezers to beak, allowing them to take it, rather than inserting the food in their mouths. But feeding them was okay the first thing in the morning and the last thing at night. They approached their food differently, depending upon whether they were taking it or it was being given. When

The Babies still enjoyed being hand-fed.

Crickets were dropped to the ground for the Babies to pick up.

They'd make a hood of their wings and descend upon their prey.

If a cricket fell, it was promptly recaptured.

a cricket or mealworm was taken from the tweezers, it would be snapped at and grabbed and, in the case of a cricket, usually shredded. The Babies' wings would quiver slightly while they would utter one muffled begging note. Grown up one minute, babies the next.

Since they both liked catching prey themselves, I would capture crickets and drop them to the ground in front of the birds. They'd wait, at times making a "hood" of their wings, until the cricket would move and then they would rapidly descend upon it. If a cricket fell, it was promptly picked up. As with the ants, the Babies would pick up a cricket somewhere below its head and, delivering that fatal blow, apparently immobilize it. Then they'd drop it, look at it, pick it up, maneuver it around in the beak until it was in the desired position for swallowing, and then devour it. Their success rate with crickets was close to 100 percent. When I would watch the male at the Pond Site—Bonnie and Ben's father—bring several bits of food back to the nestlings at one time, I wondered just how he was able to keep two or three items quiet in his beak while capturing the third or fourth. The Babies provided the answer to that query.

When they would hunt along the ground, they'd keep their tails up, wren style, and raise and lower their wings as though trying to create some air movement to blow away debris and perhaps reveal some food. The raising and lowering of the wings reminded me of a vampire. I had to wonder: why do they do it? To scare or confuse insects? To create a barrier against the clear path or escape route for an insect? Are they blocking out the sun so they might see better? Surely they are not trying to look larger for they already would seem gigantic to something as small as an insect. Are they creating a downdraft that interferes with an insect's flight? And when they were just over six weeks, they tried other forms of hunting. A little green fly was buzzing around; Bonnie watched it for a few seconds and then jumped up in mid-air and caught it. Within a week they both were hovering, she doing an excellent job in front of a spider and he, primitively, over some prey.

Although it is reported that in addition to insects, bluebird parents bring berries to their nestlings, I had not noticed that type of food being offered at the Pond Site, nor the other sites either. But lack of availability of berries early in the season, particularly for the first brood, would account for that. Nevertheless, the Babies would need to be exposed to that food which would become so important during winter. The first offering— to Ben—was a plump, ripe blueberry. He poked at it with his beak, piercing the skin, and rolled it around but didn't eat it. The next attempt was to Bonnie, and this time the berry was a mulberry. I placed a couple on a tray near the mealworms and she inspected them. Bonnie was interested and picked one up. First she shook it back and forth, then she tossed it, chased it, and shook it again before she ate it, bit by bit. She obviously liked it. After the initial taste, she returned again and again to the berries. She enjoyed the mulberries so much, she would even try to take the remaining juice off the tray. On one occasion, instead of eating a berry bite by bite, she stuffed the whole thing into her beak and then swallowed it—gulping a couple of times to help it go down. I would say that each of those mulberries is roughly one-half the size of her entire head. I also picked a few ripe black raspberries to offer her, and Bonnie liked them just as much as the mulberries. It appears that the bluebirds also ate the seeds or meats from the spruce cones, unless it was little insects that were being gleaned from them.

*I had to wonder how the Babies'
father managed to keep two or
three items quiet in his bill.*

*Tails were held high,
wren style, while hunting
along the ground.*

A tug-of-war ensues as each struggles to take possession of a bit of food.

Now the Babies would nap a couple of feet apart.

*The fledglings had
graduated to juveniles . . . Ben,*

. . . Bonnie.

The area just behind the house, including the spruce tree, apparently was their home base. When I called them one day, only Bonnie came. She didn't eat, she was quiet, called twice for her brother, and then sat there for ten to fifteen minutes waiting until she heard something overhead. When she did, her head perked up and she looked and called, getting excited when she realized he was there. She had been waiting for him to find her when he flew by and called to see whether she was in this expected spot.

Yes, behind the house was the place to reunite. It was home base. To the Babies, it was also the place where I should always be, and they had no qualms about letting me know that. The first incident came one day when they hadn't even been outdoors for two weeks. I was bent over, weeding, when all of a sudden something briefly landed on my head, took off in a circle around the top of the catalpa tree, and continued around to the weeping cherry about twenty feet behind me. It was Ben—and watching the whole thing from her perch on the weeping cherry was Bonnie. I wasn't in what they had designated as my "spot," and they wanted me to get back there.

After that, each time they would see me working in the garden, they expected me to stop, return to my "spot," and feed them. Later that day, again weeding, I looked up and saw Ben. My eyes followed him in a circle to the weeping cherry, where Bonnie sat, taking it all in. Was he showing off for her? Was he getting my attention on behalf of both of them? When I called, the Babies always called back, even when they were three hundred feet away in the woods behind the house; or they would keep in touch with me, calling just to touch base. Later that day, when I was watering the flowers in the circle, I heard one of them call. I turned around and Bonnie was in the apricot tree four or five feet away. I answered and she called again. When I said, "Hello, Baby," and called her again, she flew to the weeping cherry and answered again. She had come to get me and was showing me the way home.

As they got older and their flying skills improved, Ben would no longer just fly in to see me; he had to make a large circle and bank, perhaps do a little dip. One day I was next door at my mother's when he buzzed me, went around in a big circle, and did it again. When I realized it was Ben and started walking toward home, he flew to her clothesline and began chattering at me—hollering for me to go back to where I belong. Eventually, whenever Ben would see me in the yard, he would swoop down and circle my head while calling to me. I think it became a greeting. Most times, they'd call and make noise to let me know that they were there, but at times they were quite silent. All of a sudden, I would turn around, and there they would be on a branch, just quietly watching me and waiting for me to acknowledge them.

*In the wee hours of the morning, the Babies
returned—the molt to adult plumage had begun.*

They visited both trays.

Bonnie in the gutter—a childhood habit.

Ben on the drainpipe—another childhood habit.

There were times when one bird would steal from the other's mouth, and there were even times when a tug-of-war would ensue as each struggled to keep or take possession of some prize, such as a grasshopper. They absolutely *loved* grasshoppers. One day I managed to find two green ones (the intention being one for each bird), but they fought over them, each snatching pieces out of the other's mouth. I guess they shared; they each had two halves. But there were also times when Ben would deliberately and with obvious forethought feed Bonnie. On their fifth night out, Ben arrived at approximately seven-thirty in the evening to eat. They had almost always arrived together, but this time he was alone. I called and called to Bonnie, but received no answer. I don't know where she had been, but finally about an hour later, Ben came back, accompanied by Bonnie. He ate some mealworms, but when I gave him a cricket, he wouldn't swallow it. He kept it in his beak while dropping to the ground where Bonnie was. Her wings immediately began quivering as she opened her mouth and begged. When she did, he fed her the cricket!

The next evening, he fed her again. As mentioned, they like crickets to be given to them head down and head first. Thus far, Ben would usually maneuver the cricket in his beak until he achieved the proper position for swallowing. Now, however, if he maneuvered the cricket to a point where it was crosswise in his beak, Ben seemed to have thoughts about bringing it to her. Immediately, when she would see something in his mouth that obviously was not being swallowed, she would flutter her wings, open her beak, and peep. Does having the food perpendicular to the beak create the desire to feed? They were not even five weeks old and he had already started to feed someone else. Bonnie was never observed feeding Ben. He not only fed her but jumped at her beck and call. We've all witnessed the ritual of one bird feeding another, but is this just an amorous display or is it a response to a certain stimulus—the same one that will come into play during courtship? Ben appeared to respond to food held perpendicular to his beak, but is he the only one with an inborn need to make an offering? Bonnie showed no such tendency. Is she a princess, already in training for the time when a male will have to make all the right moves to court her fancy?

That beautiful act on Ben's part was also extended to me, at least on one occasion. Ben either wanted to feed me or show me what he had caught. He captured a spider, but instead of eating it, he hopped over to where I was sitting and gave a muffled, chattery call, all the while with the spider in his beak. When he got there, instead of eating it, he held it in his mouth, continued to call, and then jumped up on the little bench near me. Then he did it all again, but this time he jumped on my arm. He stayed for a bit watching me, but I guess when I didn't open my mouth and beg, as his sister did, he gave up, ate the spider himself, and then left.

GROWING UP

Each day their forays took the Babies a little farther from home base, exploring all the trees around, becoming braver. Every morning I would call them and their muffled little responses would seem to be farther off in the distance. By the time the Babies were seven weeks old, and had been outdoors for three weeks, I noticed that fewer crickets were being eaten. They had been finding much of their own food, and crickets probably were no longer special. Whereas they had preferred the crickets—became excited when they saw them and even enjoyed catching them—now mealworms moved to the forefront. I suppose they were more of a treat. Catching their own food; dipping, banking, and other fancy flying; explorations farther and farther from home base; expanding their horizons; and even napping a couple of feet apart during their afternoon siesta—the Babies certainly were growing up. They were no longer fledglings. They had graduated to juvenile stage. But still, when they came for treats, they'd flutter their wings and utter that soft begging sound—I suppose to me they would always be "the Babies."

BLUEBIRD FRIENDS — My mother owns property abutting mine to the south. Just behind her house on the east is a huge conifer, and to the south of her house, and bordered by split-rail fencing, is a wildflower patch that is always loaded with grasshoppers—probably thousands of them. On most nights, the Babies roosted in her conifer. Because of a couple of stray cats, I had always been afraid that they would want to hunt there, too, on that fertile ground with the perfect perch that the fencing provided. On Sunday morning, July 9, I called the Babies for a treat. They were in my mother's evergreen. I received the instant and customary vocal response, but they didn't appear for the handout. Instead, I watched them fly in and out of the tree, land on her clothesline, on her deck, on her garden bench, chimney, and roof, ignoring me and my call. Next, one of them flew to my property and sat on top of a bluebird nest box occupied by a wren. As I watched with utter surprise, an adult male bluebird—perhaps a floater with no mate of his own—went in and out of the box while one of my Babies watched him. Then the three of them flew around the box, occasionally landing, and the adult periodically went inside. All three then returned to my mother's conifer, her clothesline, and her garden seat and frolicked for about fifteen minutes more.

Eventually the Babies appeared for breakfast, but I knew that their forays away from home base would get longer and, even though they'd continue to visit me, sometimes for hours at a stretch, their dependence on me was waning. That is as it should be, and I hoped that the adult male would teach Ben to sing.

A short while later, I saw the adult male again, but this time he was accompanied by a second bird, either a female or a juvenile. Perhaps he was not a floater as I had suspected. I watched as my two followed them. Might they hook up with a bluebird family after all? Adult bluebirds would be more inclined to embrace them into the family unit than run them out. When the Babies came back about one-half hour later, they visited the tray and devoured several mealworms. Bonnie had a cricket. They were there only a few minutes. Ben picked up a mealworm and kept it in his mouth, the way he would when he was going to feed Bonnie, and they left. They stopped at the weeping cherry for a moment, and I could still see the mealworm held crosswise in his beak. Then they took off in the same direction as when they followed that male. Had he enlisted their aid in caring for his family?

Still later, the adult male appeared with what I now could tell was an adult female. They were at the weeping cherry together, but soon flew to the nest box to inspect it. Perhaps they were both floaters—it seemed a bit late to start a second brood, although prior nest failure could be a factor. There were two unoccupied nest boxes on my mother's property in an area that is more open, with better hunting possibilities, but the pair seemed to prefer this, in spite of the fact that it was occupied by a wren.

After that I saw less of the Babies. In bad weather they would stay huddled together in the spruce tree, play in the gutter even in the rain, eat, snooze, and just hang around, at times for four or five hours at a clip. But generally their visits were reduced to two or three a day, and they spent the majority of their time away from home and out of earshot. Whether or not they were with that bluebird family is unknown.

A VALUABLE LESSON — By July 12, the Babies' days of carefree youth were over. Until then, in spite of all that had happened around them, they had lived charmed lives. It was about eight o'clock in the morning. The babies had spent around two hours with me, eating, snoozing, playing together in the spruce tree and the gutter. It was time to do something else—whatever it is that they do when they disappear for hours at a stretch, perhaps look up that bluebird family or just hunt in other places.

First one left the spruce tree for the catalpa and called to its sibling. I don't remember who left first, although it generally was Bonnie. Within a minute, the other followed. I figured we'd see each other again later; I went inside for a cup of coffee. I don't know how long I was in the house, but it couldn't have been more than a few minutes when I heard a commotion among the birds outside. I knew that sound: birds were scurrying and hollering; a hawk was around. Thus far, their interaction with other species consisted of Bonnie's sitting very intently next to a house finch just looking at her, watching in almost a timid way as a robin called and called, probably to its young, and staring at a woodpecker. I dashed back outside in time to see birds scattering in all directions and something rush into the spruce. That "something" was a bluejay who now was motionless, just waiting it out.

I didn't see the Babies anywhere. When the hiding subsided and birds resumed their activity, I began calling the Babies. There was no answer. I called them intermittently throughout the day, but there was still no answer. They were so inexperienced in such matters. . . I was so sure the hawk had gotten one of them.

There was one thing that puzzled me, however. A hawk wouldn't take both of them. Where was the other bird? After a time it should come out of hiding and look for its sibling or something to eat. When hours had passed, I contemplated many possibilities. In absolute fear, the other bird might have flown into something—a building, a tree trunk—and broken its neck. I felt so sad, but I dutifully continued calling them. I am usually the optimist, but this was different. So many hours had gone by with not so much as a call to one another. I was convinced that they had been in the wrong place at the wrong time.

Just about eleven hours later—around seven o'clock, while I was watering the garden—I thought I had heard the muffled call of a bluebird. I dropped what I had been doing and returned to the home base area. Neither of the Babies was there, but again I heard one of them call. This time it was the "soft call," the one that can be heard only from less than ten feet. I looked around and there was Ben, sitting on one of the lower branches of the catalpa. He appeared frightened and quiet. I was sure that he was hungry. As I moved toward the house to get the tweezers and crickets, Ben followed me to the spruce. He was not his lively self. He ate, but then just sat there. I know that it is not considered appropriate to attribute human emotions to birds and animals, but I just can't help it: the body language, the posture, the behavior—there is no other word to describe the way he looked and acted than *sad*. He didn't call his sister; he didn't bounce around; he wasn't his usual bubbly self—he just sat. After about twenty minutes of just sitting there blankly, he moved to the weeping cherry and began calling to his sister. There was no response. I was sure that the hawk had gotten Bonnie, and I thought over and over about the things they did together—about Ben feeding her, about how they slept together, cuddled, warbled, and I felt so sorry for him. After several minutes Ben moved to the evergreen at my mother's, and I resumed my watering.

About eight o'clock I again heard a bluebird call and responded. The bird went directly to the catalpa and called again. It appeared to be Bonnie, but I had to get close to be sure. It was Bonnie, and within a minute or two, Ben joined us. Now both of them had that frightened, cautious look about them and neither was truly relaxed, but they ate, cricket after cricket and mealworm upon mealworm. She even dropped down to the ground, landed on my foot, and proceeded to pick something up from the grass near my feet. I talked softly to them and they enjoyed it, cocking and pulling their heads forward, just staring at me and listening. They began to look a bit more relaxed. As the sun set and it turned darker, they left to roost for the night.

Apparently they had learned a valuable lesson. No doubt they were frightened and may have even been hiding since the morning. I couldn't help but think of how hard life is, not only for all birds but particularly for Bonnie and Ben, because they were orphaned, abandoned, and vulnerable and now had to make it basically on their own.

The next morning the birds in the yard were rather subdued, which indicated to me that a hawk had again been present. And so I didn't see the Babies until that evening, again around seven o'clock, but this time they didn't act frightened. Because I provide so amply all year for birds here, the yard is quite a fertile hunting ground for sharp-shinned hawks, particularly in winter. If the Babies spend their days elsewhere, it might be best for them. I saw them much less after they followed the other bluebirds that one day, and now it would be less yet. It was obvious that they had become self-sufficient juveniles. I had to wonder what they did with their days. Had they been recruited to help out? If they had new friends, I wished they would bring them around.

NATURE CALLS — The Babies didn't sleep in my mother's conifer that night. Instead, I watched them go into a white pine on the east end of her property about four hundred feet away.

The second morning after the hawk incident, the Babies were in the yard bright and early, and I thought everything would be back to "normal." They ate, relaxed, and snoozed on a branch of the spruce, just as they had been doing all along. Suddenly they both looked up and began calling—very unusual as all three of us were together. I could hear a bluebird overhead and the Babies left. A day or two earlier, I thought I had heard another bluebird while the Babies visited with me, but at the time dismissed it. For the next few days, perhaps out of loyalty since they no longer needed my assistance or maybe to considerately wean me, the Babies would visit only once or twice each day, and frequently afterward they could be seen at the very top of a tree, calling to their adopted family and waiting for a return call before departing. Soon they appeared only in the morning. They'd eat, they'd visit, they'd be beckoned and leave. Finally one morning, they only called to me from the treetops. I responded, but they didn't come down. They either were saying "hello" or "good-bye," or wanted me to follow them. After that I was sure they were gone for good. I was convinced they had been interacting with those bluebirds that were in the garden that day. Just how, I wasn't sure—although it seems likely that they had been recruited to help raise a family. But that, too, would be in their best interest, as they could hone their hunting and nesting skills and learn the fine art of singing, all under the auspices of savvy adults.

In the wee hours of the morning, almost two weeks later, the Babies appeared again. They obviously no longer needed me, and if they had come only to eat, they could have gone directly to the tray and helped themselves to some mealworms. Instead, they called until I came out of the house. They had not forgotten me and wanted to see me—I think they missed me. A bond remained between us, and even after an absence of nearly two weeks, Ben—who had begun to show some rust at the edges of the breast—still wanted me to pass him the mealworms with the tweezers. And when he had his fill, he brought some to his sister—just like old times. Predictably, Bonnie remained friendly but aloof—she'd "talk" to me but no longer wanted me to feed her. Either Ben fed her or she'd feed herself. They visited both trays —the one on the deck and the one on the ground—but apparently wanted to retain some habits from their "childhood," even reverting to playing in the gutter and, that first habit that they had formed, landing on the drainpipe. After that, they visited regularly again, even for three or four hours at a stretch. Of course, the moment they were summoned from above, they departed.

Their unique and loving relationship continued and remained very obvious in all that they did. Apparently Ben felt very protective of his sister and, in addition to making sure she received her fair share of food, behaved as though he would defend her from danger. One morning when they were visiting, Ben at the ground tray and Bonnie in the tree, a squirrel entered the yard and began poking around under the spruce about three feet from Ben. Apparently aware of the limited danger potential, he watched the squirrel but didn't leave the tray or stop eating, as he would have had a cat been lurking about. However, when the squirrel ran up the tree, Ben became concerned and flew after him, positioning himself between his sister and the squirrel. Bonnie moved away from the squirrel and Ben remained by her side.

What a coincidence—the length of their disappearance, between their daily and two-week absences, conveniently covered the amount of time necessary to fledge a nestful of babies. I'm sure they learned much while they were gone, and I consider their rehabilitation and release a success. Score one for the bluebirds!

YESTERDAY,
TODAY, AND TOMORROW

Just the other day, as I was weeding, Ben swooped down in a circle in front of me. It was his lovable greeting. I felt a smile deep within and began to reminisce. I thought back to the very first bluebirds that I saw as a child and how impressed I had been by their beauty. I remembered the first bluebirds to appear in my garden so long ago and how they teased me with their appearance at the nest box, leaving me wanting them to nest here even more. Then I thought about all the beautiful bluebirds that I had watched raise their families this year and, finally, about the two little balls of fluff—Bonnie and Ben— temporarily on loan to me from nature, whom I had come to know in such an intimate and enriching way.

The Babies have become adults now, world-wise and self-sufficient. This year I'll keep a supply of mealworms and berries, and let some pokeweed and sumac grow, should favorable conditions exist and they decide to stay the winter. If they don't, I shall anxiously await the next nesting season, when Bonnie and Ben, my personal harbingers of spring, return to start another new chapter in their lives.

This truly has been a very bluebird summer, indeed.

Appendix I

LANDSCAPING FOR BLUEBIRDS

If you live in an area potentially inhabited by bluebirds—a rural area—figure them and their requirements into your landscaping plans. Create a summer nesting habitat and provide a winter refuge. During the nesting season, bluebirds need a place to raise a family and habitat for hunting—a large, open area with perches—perhaps some small trees or shrubs that will double later on as berry producers. Winter concerns for the bluebird are food, shelter, and water.

Landscaping is done in levels: canopy, understory, shrubs and vines, and grasses and forbs, the latter which constitute the "open area." Open areas may be either mowed or not, but bluebirds *love* newly mowed lawns. Unmowed open areas generally have some wildflowers that attract the insects that hide among the grasses. Occasional mowing or regular partial mowing reveals those insects to the bluebirds, who eat some themselves and feed some to their babies. Ideally, the open area should be surrounded by tall trees and vines to offer shelter to both fledglings and adults.

In addition to providing food, shelter, and nesting sites for birds and other wildlife, tall trees play another important role in the garden. The high shade cast by the canopy protects tender understory trees and shrubs from too much sun or wind. Tall trees moderate the summer temperatures and, with their leaf litter, improve the condition of the soil. Evergreens moderate not only cold winter temperatures but wind chill as well. So it is desirable to have evergreens as well as deciduous trees in the garden, for beside food production, they provide winter shelter.

Tall trees, unfortunately, take several years to grow to a useful height and many more years to reach maturity. While it is wise to plan for the future, you must work with what is available and then add the bluebird essentials. For example, oaks are deep-rooted trees that produce an acid ground litter. Thus, shade-loving understory trees preferring an acid soil, such as flowering dogwood, make excellent companion plants. On the fringes of the shade cast by the oak, blueberries may be planted to receive part sun, part shade and acid soil; and Virginia creeper, tolerant of most conditions, may be planted to climb the oak. Such a grouping would provide fruits or berries at different levels from summer on.

The secret to successful gardening with native plants is to choose those that grow in your area naturally or whose habitats can be duplicated in your garden without too much alteration. Choosing the appropriate plants for a region results in lower maintenance, ultimately. Determine your natural environment in conjunction with its level of hardiness or aspect of climate to ascertain what will grow best in your garden. Select trees and/or shrubs that will provide food for an extended period, some whose berries will mature in fall and winter and remain on the trees or shrubs as long as possible. The most critical period is winter through spring.

Following this commentary is a list of plants beneficial to the bluebird, grouped by level from tall trees down to vines and herbaceous perennials. Some careful planning of the garden at all levels will provide ample food and shelter for bluebirds (as well as other wildlife) and could turn your garden into a bluebird paradise.

The only element that remains is water for bathing and drinking, and that is the final touch to birdscaping. We are not all fortunate enough to have a stream running across our property, but running water from either an artificial waterfall or pond setup or a drip system attached to the birdbath can take care of that. Absent running water, a small submersible heater designed for use with plastic or concrete birdbaths is inexpensive and simple to use, and it will keep water liquid even during extended periods of subfreezing temperatures.

Table 1
Tall Trees (more than 30 feet)[*]

Name	Size	Season	Habitat	Notes
Celtis laevigata C. occidentalis (Sugarberry, hackberry)	80 50–90	Fall– winter	Sun to light shade on moist, neutral to alkaline soils. *C. laevigata* grows in Zones 6–9 and is hardy to −10°; *C. occidentalis* grows in Zones 3–10 and is hardy to −30°.	Sugarberry growth is moderate, trees are deep rooted; the fruits are small, dry, and sweet.
Ilex opaca (American holly)	40–50	Late fall– spring	Versatile, growing in acid soils on most habitats in Zones 6–9.	Shallow-rooted, broad-leafed evergreen with dark green, glossy, and spiny leaves; red (sometimes yellow or orange) berries appear on female trees. Good companion plants are dogwood and blueberries.
Juniperus virginiana (Eastern red cedar)	40–50	Fall– winter	Sunny locations on dry to moist, neutral to alkaline soils in Zones 3–9.	Aromatic evergreen with blue fruits; berries are sweet and juicy. A good companion plant is sparkleberry (*Vaccinum arboreum*).

*Hardiness based on USDA Plant Hardiness Zones; size is noted for mature plants.

Table 1 *(continued)*

Name	Size	Season	Habitat	Notes
Morus rubra *M. alba* (Red, white mulberry)	40–60	Summer	Moist soils in sunny locations; mulberries are hardy to –20°.	Fast growth; juicy, edible, multiple fruits attractive to many birds and other wildlife.
Nyssa sylvatica (Black gum, tupelo, sour gum)	50–75	Fall	Sun or light shade on dry, acid soils in Zones 5–8.	Fast growing.
Prunus virginiana *P. serotina* (Chokecherry, black cherry)	80 50	Late summer	Grows well in Zones 4–8, any soil or exposure.	Widespread; fruit slightly bitter, pulp juicy.
Sassafras albidum (Sassafras)	100	Summer–fall	Hardy to Zone 5.	Fast growth rate; fruits and cavities attractive to bluebirds.

Table 2
Small Trees (less than 30 feet)*

Name	Size	Season	Habitat	Notes
Amelanchier arborea *A. canadensis* (Serviceberry, shadbush, shadblow, Juneberry)	15–25 30	Summer	Grows on moist, neutral to acid soils on rocky slopes and balds in eastern North America. Does well in either sun or part shade. Both species hardy to –30° (Zones 4–8).	Moderate growth rate; fruit is dry to juicy and sweet.
Cornus florida and other spp. (Flowering dogwood, et al.)	20–30	Fall– winter	Does best in part shade on moist, neutral to acid soils. Native woodland tree grows in Zones 5–8.	Beautiful and graceful, popular ornamental, extensively planted for its beauty during spring flowering season.
Crataegus phaenopyrum (Washington hawthorn)	25	Fall– spring	Does best on sunny sites with moist, well-drained soils. Hardy to –20° (Zones 5–9).	Small red fruits.
Elaeagnus umbellata *E. augustifolia* (Autumn olive; Russian olive)	20	Fall– winter	Sunny locations; average to dry conditions, any soil.	Moderate to fast growth; fruit is berrylike with mealy, sweet, edible pulp. *Elaeagnus spp.* are tolerant of cold, drought, and pollution and may be grown as either a small tree or shrub.

*Hardiness based on USDA Plant Hardiness Zones; size is noted for mature plants.

Table 2 (continued)

Name	Size	Season	Habitat	Notes
Ilex decidua (Possumhaw, winterberry) *I. laevigata* (Winterberry)	20–30	Early fall– spring	Prefers moist soils, full sun; hardy Zones 6–8.	Needs several freeze-thaw cycles to make fruit palatable; unattractive to starlings. Orange to red berries ripen in September, at times lasting until April.
Malus spp. (Crabapples)	25	Late summer– spring	Does well under most conditions, needs well-drained soils. Hardiness varies, all need winter chill.	Popular for the beauty of its spring bloom. Fruits eaten by many birds and other wildlife.
Myrica cerifera (Wax myrtle, Southern bayberry)	15–20	Fall– winter	Deep, wet, or dry, acid soil; sun or part shade. Hardy to −20° (Zones 6–9).	Fast-growing, aromatic, broad-leafed evergreen with pale blue, waxy berries on female trees.
Prunus pensylvanica *P. virginiana* (Pin cherry; chokecherry)	30 20	Summer	Both species are very hardy and grow best on moist soils in sunny locations.	Fruits of both species have bitter pulp.
Rhamnus caroliniana (Carolina buckthorn)	30	Late summer– winter	Moist, neutral soils; grows in Zones 7–9.	

Table 2 (continued)

Name	Size	Season	Habitat	Notes
Sorbus americana (Mountain ash)	30	Fall–winter	Hardiness varies but definitely needs a winter chill; does best in Zones 3–6. Grows best on moist but well-drained soils in sunny locations.	Red, apple-like fruits have a bitter pulp.
Vaccinum arboreum (Sparkleberry)	20–30	Fall–winter	Grows best on dry, sandy to rocky, neutral to acid soils in sunny locations. Hardy in Zones 6–9.	This is the tallest of the blueberries; fruit has a sweet pulp with large seeds.

Table 3
Shrubs*

Name	Size	Season	Habitat	Notes
Aronia arbutifolia (Red chokeberry)	8	Fall–winter	Moist soils, hardy to Zones 4–9.	White flowers followed by clusters of glossy, red fruits all during fall and winter.
Ilex glabra (Inkberry; winterberry)	8–10	Fall–winter	Sun to part shade on sandy, moist, acid soils; grows in Zones 5–9; *I. verticillata* is hardy to Zone 4 and drought tolerant.	Berries on female plants; forms thickets.
Ilex verticillata (Winterberry)	15	Fall–winter	Grows best in full sun to part shade on moist, acid soils; is hardy to Zone 4.	Produces an abundance of red berries along the stems on female plants.
Myrica pensylvanica (Northern bayberry)	8	Fall–winter	Grows in Zones 5–9 on sandy soils.	Deciduous to evergreen.
Pyracantha coccinea (Firethorn)	8	Fall–winter	Prefers full sun, well-drained soil; hardy to Zones 4 and 5 (depending on the cultivar).	Thorny semi-evergreen to evergreen ornamental shrub with brilliant berries starting in September.

*Hardiness based on USDA Plant Hardiness Zones; size is noted for mature plants.

Table 3 *(continued)*

Name	Size	Season	Habitat	Notes
Rhus copallina *R. glabra* *R. typhina* (Dwarf, smooth, and staghorn sumacs)	25 20 15–30	All late summer–spring	Tolerant of various conditions; *R. typhina* hardy to −40°; others a little less hardy.	Sumacs may form thickets, are very widespread, and are frequently considered weeds; fruit is sour. Sumacs may become small trees.
Rosa multiflora (Multiflora rose)	6–15	Fall–winter	Found along roadsides and at the border of woods and fields from southern New England, south; tolerant of a variety of conditions.	Attractive small white flowers in late spring; forms impenetrable thickets.
Rubus spp. (Blackberries, raspberries)	8	Summer	Prefers rich, moist soil in sunny locations; hardy to Zone 3.	Fast growing, deciduous; forms thickets.
Sambucus canadensis (American elder)	16	Late summer	Wet conditions; hardy to Zone 4.	The berries are dark, juicy, and slightly sweet on this widespread, thicket-forming shrub.
Symphoricarpos albus (Snowberry)	4	Fall–winter	Does well in shade, poor soil; hardy Zones 3–7.	Waxy, white, berry-like drupe.

Table 3 (continued)

Name	Size	Season	Habitat	Notes
Vaccinum spp. (Blueberry)	3–15	Summer– fall	Prefers moist, well-drained, acid soil, sun to light shade; hardy in Zones 4–7.	White, urn-shaped flowers in May are followed by delicious fruits in summer. Highbush blueberries are tall growing (to 15 ft.), lowbush blueberries only grow to 2–3 ft.
Viburnum dentatum (Arrowwood)	5–15	Fall	*V. dentatum* grows best on moist to dry, acid to very acid soils in Zones 6–9.	Berries are blue to black and juicy.
Viburnum nudum (Possumhaw)	16		Zones 5–9.	
Viburnum prunifolium (Blackhaw)	5–15		Zones 4–9.	

Table 4
Vines and Herbaceous Perennials*

Name	Size	Season	Habitat	Notes
Celastrus scandens (Climbing bittersweet)	Vine	Fall–winter	Found in thickets and woods; hardy to Zone 2; fruits best in full sun.	Rapidly growing deciduous vine with showy orange-red berries on female plants from October; very widespread and can be invasive.
Lonicera spp. (Honeysuckles)	Vine	Fall–winter	Sunny to partly sunny locations; most conditions.	Showy, vigorous, summer-blooming vines; *L. japonica* et al. may become invasive.
Parthenocissus quinquefolia (Virginia creeper)	Vine	Fall–winter	Hardy to Zone 3; tolerant of various conditions.	Vigorous deciduous vine, blue-black berries; good red fall color.
Phytolacca americana (Pokeweed, pokeberry)	to 10 ft.	Summer–fall	Any conditions, Zones 4–10.	Dark purple, long-lasting, and abundant berries in drooping clusters are poisonous.
Rhus radicans (Poison ivy)	Vine	Late summer–winter	Grows throughout under all conditions.	White berry-like clusters. All parts of the plant contain a skin irritant; berries popular with birds and other wildlife.

*Hardiness based on USDA Plant Hardiness Zones; size is noted for mature plants.

Table 4 (*continued*)

Name	Size	Season	Habitat	Notes
Vitus vulpina (Wild grape, fox grape)	Vine	Fall	Grows on river-banks and bottomlands; prefers moist, well-drained soil in sun to light shade; hardy in Zones 5–9.	Vine climbs by tendrils; small greenish flowers in late spring to early summer are followed by shiny black grapes that become sweet after a frost; many species of birds eat wild grapes.

THE ABCS OF NEST BOXES

To a bluebird, the single most important feature in choosing a nesting site is its location. That means, first, the right habitat and second, orientation. Bluebirds are creatures of open habitats, whether they are backyards, fields, farms, orchards, golf courses, or cemeteries. So the first consideration should be locating the box in an open area. Ideally, there should be some perches nearby from which to hunt, and the entrance to the box should face some trees or shrubs, for the young will need a target when they are ready to fledge. The opening to the nest box should be away from the direction of storms. In the Northeast, most summer storms come from the south, rarely from the east, so it is desirable to have the opening oriented toward the east.

Probably less important to the bluebirds themselves but equally important to their success, is dimensions—the bluebirds at the Road Site have nested successfully in nonstandard boxes for years. Traditionally, bluebirds have used cavities excavated by other birds and, therefore, dimensions might vary quite a bit from one nest to the next. A large cavity will make extra and unnecessary work for the female when she constructs her nest, although it must be at least large enough to accommodate the average-size clutch. Local bluebird advocate Evelyn Rifenburg praises the success rate achieved with the Peterson box, which is conical in shape. This type of box, with its tapered bottom, certainly requires much less gathering of nesting materials.

Nest box monitoring is an important aspect of bluebird stewardship. Records may or may not be kept—that is one of the finer points of bluebirding—but monitoring is integral to success. Putting up a nest box and not monitoring it may be compared to starting a vegetable garden and then not watering it. In some years the rain will take care of the garden amply, but in most years it won't. You can become as involved as you like—some folks have made bluebirding a full-time avocation. The North American Bluebird Society, with its local chapters, is an excellent organization to join. Their address is Box 6295, Silver Spring, Maryland 20906-0295.

The tables that follow cover the basics: suggested nest box specifications, a typical nesting timetable, and a list of competitors and predators.

SAMPLE NEST BOX

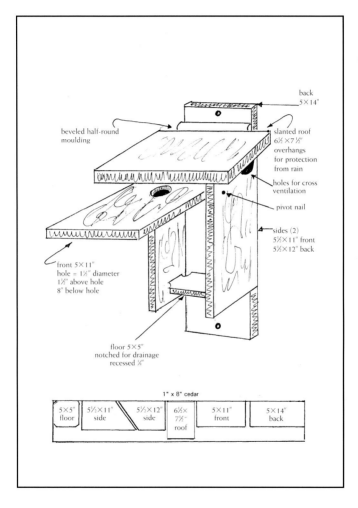

back
5×14″

beveled half-round
moulding

slanted roof
6½″×7½″
overhangs
for protection
from rain

holes for cross
ventilation

pivot nail

sides (2)
5½×11″ front
5½×12″ back

front 5×11″
hole = 1⅛″ diameter
1½″ above hole
8″ below hole

floor 5×5″
notched for drainage
recessed ⅛″

1″ x 8″ cedar

5×5″ floor	5½×11″ side	5½×12″ side	6½×7½″ roof	5×11″ front	5×14″ back

Table 5
Constructing, Installing, and Maintaining the Nest Box

Material
5' piece of 1 × 8" cedar (assuming an average blade size of ⅟₁₆" for noncarbide tipped blades)

The actual thickness of a 1" piece of lumber is ¾". This thickness allows for insulation from both heat during summer nesting and cold during winter roosting. Cedar is a good wood for use outdoors and does not have to be painted. The rough side of the board should be used on the inside of the front of the box, or the inside should be grooved to give footing to nestlings ready to fledge.

Floor
5 × 5"

The floor should be notched at the corners for drainage and recessed ⅜".

Sides (2)
5½ × 12" for the back, and 5½ × 11" for the front

The sides should be 1" higher in the back than the front to accommodate the slanted roof that facilitates rain runoff. Place pivot nail low enough so door doesn't hit roof.

Back
5 × 14"

Drill holes at top and bottom and through pipe at corresponding distances for pole mounting.

Roof
6½ × 7½"
(wider is better)

It is very important that the nest stay dry at all times. The roof's overhang protects the inside from rain as well as sun. The ends of the roof should be cut at an angle, especially the rear part as it may then sit flush against the back. A piece of half-round molding, beveled to fit where the roof meets the back, should be used to seal the seam between the roof and the back, or flashing or a sealing compound may be utilized instead.

Entry hole
1½" diameter

The hole should be 1½" diameter for the Eastern bluebird (1⁹⁄₁₆" in areas inhabited by Western or mountain bluebirds). There should be 1⅛" above the hole and 8" between the hole and the bottom. A predator guard consisting of an extra thickness of wood can be added around the hole; it can be made from the leftover wood.

Table 5 (*continued*)

Mounting	The box should be mounted to pipe strong enough and buried deeply enough to hold the box without swaying (two to three feet is good). The entry hole should face some shrubs or small trees as a landing target for babies' maiden flights, but the hole should face away from the direction of summer (and winter) storms. The box should be mounted, if possible, 75–100' away from trees and about 5' above the ground. Boxes thus mounted are less favored by sparrows. To keep the boxes as safe as possible from predators, mount on pole with a stovepipe predator guard as illustrated in *Bird Watcher's Digest*, "Enjoying Bluebirds More."
Maintenance	Unless birds start a new nest directly on top of the old, nesting material should be removed, as the pair may be reluctant to use it again and may look elsewhere. When the season is over, the box should be cleaned out, and before the spring season, scrubbed with a brush dipped in water and bleach.
Monitoring	Monitoring is an important part of bluebirding. The degree to which boxes are monitored is an individual preference. It is not necessary to log every little detail, although it is a good idea for later comparative purposes. Follow the "Typical Nesting Timetable" for information to record. But whether information is logged or not, the age of the chicks should be determined and monitoring should at least be done for signs of blowfly and other predators, insect infestation, tampering (whether by undesirable competitors or humans), and general condition of the nest and babies (e.g., whether nest has gotten wet, whether there are any dead chicks) or any other problems. It is just as important not to monitor after the chicks are twelve days old.

Table 6

A Typical
Nesting Timetable*

March 20	Male has returned and located a site to offer female.
March 21–April 4	Female accepts site and male.
April 5–April 16	Female builds nest.
April 17–April 21	Honeymoon.
April 22–April 25	Female lays eggs (one per day for an average clutch size of four).
April 26–May 9	Incubation.
May 9	Eggs hatch; chicks' eyes are sealed shut, sparse tufts of natal down are visible on bright coral skin.
May 9–May 12	Skin of wings, head, back look bluish as feathers develop underneath it.
May 13–May 15	Feather sheaths begin to emerge on wings.
May 15	First feathers burst from tips of sheaths; brooding stops.
May 16–May 19	Eyes are fully opened.
May 20	The young are active in the nest.
May 21–May 28	Fledging and first flight.
May 28–June 2	Fledglings remain hidden, are fed and protected by parents.
June 3	Fledglings now follow parents.
June 4	Fledglings feed unassisted.
Second brood	Any time after fledging of first brood female will prepare nest for a second brood while the male continues to care for fledglings; when the new young hatch, juveniles from first brood assist in feeding their younger brothers and sisters.

*Based upon average weather and climate for the Mid-Hudson Valley region, New York; north or south of this point, adjust dates accordingly.

Table 7
Nest Box Competitors

Material Found in Nest Box	Competitor	Combative Action
Nest of woven grasses surrounded by white feathers; 4–6 white eggs	Tree swallow	Install a second box, 15–20′ away. The swallow and the bluebird hunt at different levels and the tree swallow is a friendly competitor who often will defend both its own and the bluebird box.
Large nest of sticks and twigs; 6–8 white eggs speckled with brown	House wren	Place boxes designed for wrens near shrubs on the periphery of the open area. The pesky wren will build decoy nests but use only one; it may destroy bluebird eggs and young. This year, when the swallows had finished nesting, the wrens entered their box and removed all the nesting material.
Very large nest with a mixture of grass, weeds, seed heads, feathers, paper, straw, and junk; 5–6 gray-white eggs speckled with brown	English (or house) sparrow	Sparrows are the bluebirds' number one enemy and thus the most undesirable competitor. Sparrows may be humanely captured and removed from the area, or their nesting material may be repeatedly removed until they move on. Sparrows ruin bluebird eggs and young, and may even peck an incubating female to death. To discourage sparrows from using nest boxes, mount nest boxes low to the ground (3–5′), keep them away from buildings, and select ones with a smaller bottom. The only foolproof way to eliminate sparrows, however, is to remove male birds from the area.

Where natural cavities are used for nesting, starlings are the bluebird's number one enemy, but they are not a problem when nest boxes are used and the entry hole is 1½″ in diameter. Size precludes their entry, but starlings remain a strong competitor when it comes to winter food supplies.

Beside tree swallows, chickadees and white-breasted nuthatches are among the native species that compete with bluebirds for nesting cavities. These birds are also beneficial and frequently face the same problems as bluebirds. It is kind to accommodate them as well. Their preferred dimensions may be found in other publications, although they will use dimensions outlined for bluebirds.

Table 8
Nest Box Predators

Signs	Predator	Remedial Action
Incubating female, eggs or young gone; nest material pulled out and lying on ground, or feathers on the ground, scratch marks on the post.	Ground predator (raccoon, cat, opossum)	Use stovepipe predator baffle.
Nestlings' heads scabby; development slow, larvae attached to young, brown pupal capsules in bottom of box.	Bluebird blowfly (*Protocalliphora sialia*)	The parasitic blowfly preys on bluebirds at night and is thus unnoticed during cursory daytime inspections of the nest box. The nest proper should be checked by slipping a putty knife underneath and looking for the telltale signs. Although a mild infestation generally causes little harm to the chicks, heavy infestations (which are more likely to occur with the later broods) can severely weaken the nestlings. The larvae should be removed. If there is a heavy infestation, the nesting material should be discarded and replaced with fresh, *dry* material—it should be fashioned in the same shape, with a cup. After Day 12, the nest box should not be opened, as it may push the nestlings to fledge prematurely. Some bluebird enthusiasts do not recommend monitoring the boxes at all, since human scent around the nesting area may attract snakes. This may be averted, however, with the proper use of a predator baffle.
Undisturbed nest, some or all eggs or young missing; no scratch marks, no mess in the nest box or on the ground around it.	Snake	Use stovepipe predator baffle.
	Crow, jay, grackle	Install wooden predator guard over entrance hole and/or lower nesting material to keep it farther from the hole.

Appendix III

A WINTER RECIPE

Evergreens offer daytime shelter during inclement weather and winterized nest or roosting boxes are in place for evenings. Berries are ripe and ready to be eaten, but it's cold outside and you'd like to provide just a little bit more.

Mealworms may be supplied in a bluebird feeder or on a tray—they are full of protein—or a palatable and beneficial peanut butter and cornmeal mixture may be offered. As mentioned earlier, just about all birds love this concoction, taking it for themselves and feeding it to their young. It makes an excellent winter supplement, giving proteins and fats. It's easy to prepare and the ingredients are readily available.

3-pound can vegetable shortening, such as Crisco

2 cups peanut butter (creamy or chunky)

5 pounds white flour

2 24-ounce containers cornmeal

Melt the shortening in a large pot until it is liquid, taking care not to allow it to burn.

Add the peanut butter and allow to melt thoroughly, stirring until blended. Add the flour and stir until blended, then add the cornmeal and stir.

Pack into plastic containers about the size of a suet holder and freeze, or stuff into milk cartons and refrigerate to be later cut into slices. Or refrigerate the mixture in large containers and scrape out by the spoonful for placement on a picnic bench, table, or platform feeder. How long the mixture lasts depends upon the number of birds being fed.

NOTE: Other goodies such as raisins, currants, or sunflower or peanut hearts may be added to the mixture.